W9-CER-596

the complete

girls of grace

devotional and Bible study workbook

Point of Grace

HOWARD BOOKS
A DIVISION OF SIMON & SCHUSTER
New York   London   Toronto   Sydney

2 Books in 1: *Girls of Grace* and *Girls of Grace, Make It Real*

Our purpose at Howard Books is to:

- *Increase faith* in the hearts of growing Christians
- *Inspire holiness* in the lives of believers
- *Instill hope* in the hearts of struggling people everywhere

Because He's coming again!

Published by Howard Books, a division of Simon & Schuster, Inc.
1230 Avenue of the Americas, New York, NY 10020

HOWARD
BOOKS

Girls Of Grace © 2002 by Point of Grace
Make It Real © 2005 by Point of Grace

All rights reserved, including the right to reproduce this book or portions thereof in any form whatsoever. For information, address Howard Subsidiary Rights Department, 1230 Avenue of the Americas, New York, NY 10020.

ISBN-13: 978-1-4391-1005-8
ISBN-10:   1-4391-1005-0

10 9 8 7 6 5

HOWARD and colophon are registered trademarks of Simon & Schuster, Inc.

Manufactured in the United States of America

For information regarding special discounts for bulk purchases, please contact Simon & Schuster Special Sales at 1-800-456-6798 or business@simonandschuster.com.

Girls of Grace
Study Guides by Whitney Prosperi • Edited by Philis Boultinghouse • Interior design by Stephanie Denney
Cover design by LinDee Loveland • Cover photos by Robert Ascroft/Industrie Rep

Photography on pages 1, 41, 51, 97, 105, 147, 189 by Robert Ascroft/Industrie Rep • Photography on pages 23, 87 by Michael Haber

Scripture quotations marked NIV are taken from *The Holy Bible, New International Version®*, copyright © 1973, 1978, 1984 by the International Bible Society. Used by permission of Zondervan Publishing House. Scripture quotations marked NASB are taken from the *New American Standard Bible®*, copyright © 1960, 1962, 1963, 1968, 1971, 1972, 1973, 1975, 1977, 1995 by the Lockman Foundation. Used by permission. Scripture quotations marked NLT are taken from the *Holy Bible, New Living Translation*, copyright © 1996. Used by permission of Tyndale House Publishers, Inc., Wheaton, Illinois 50189. Scripture quotations marked NKJV are taken from *The Holy Bible, New King James Version*, © 1982 by Thomas Nelson, Inc. Italics in Scripture quotations were added by the authors for emphasis.

Excerpt in chapter 1: Donald Whitney, Spiritual Disciplines for the Christian Life (Colorado Springs: NavPress, 1997), 15–16. Used by permission. All rights reserved.

Make It Real
Study guides by Whitney Prosperi • Edited by Philis Boultinghouse
Interior design by John Mark Luke Designs • Cover design by LinDee Loveland • Cover photo by Aaron Rapoport

Unless otherwise indicated, Scripture quotations are from the *Holy Bible, New International Version®*. Copyright © 1973, 1978, 1984 by International Bible Society. Used by permission of Zondervan. All rights reserved. Scriptures marked NKJV are taken from the *New King James Version®*. Copyright © 1982 by Thomas Nelson, Inc. Used by permission. All rights reserved. Scriptures marked NLT are taken from the *Holy Bible, New Living Translation*, copyright © 1996. Used by permission of Tyndale House Publishers, Inc., Wheaton, Illinois 60189. All rights reserved. Scriptures marked NCV are taken from the *New Century Version®*. Copyright © 1987, 1988, 1991 by Thomas Nelson, Inc. Used by permission. All rights reserved. Scriptures marked GW are taken from GOD'S WORD translation of the Bible. GOD'S WORD is a copyrighted work of God's Word to the Nations. Quotations are used by permission. Copyright 1995 by God's Word to the Nations. All rights reserved. Scriptures marked NASB are taken from the *New American Standard Bible®*. Copyright © 1960, 1962, 1963, 1968, 1971, 1972, 1973, 1975, 1977, 1995 by The Lockman Foundation. Used by permission. Scriptures marked The Message are taken from *The Message* by Eugene H. Peterson. Copyright © 1993, 1994, 1995, 1996, 2000, 2001, 2002. Used by permission of NavPress Publishing Group. All rights reserved. Italics in Scripture quotations were added by the authors for emphasis.

point of grace

girls of grace

devotional and Bible study workbook

faith, family, friends, and b♥ys

Contents

> *I entrust you to God and the word of*
> *his grace—his message that is able*
> *to build you up and give you an inheritance*
> *with all those he has set apart for himself.*
> Acts 20:32 NLT

Foreword by Beth Moore

What a perfect time to share a few words about my sisters in Point of Grace! I had the opportunity to minister with them only last night. As we "gathered 'round the river," my memory rewound an entire decade to the very same church where I first saw them. Long before "Point of Grace" was a household name in countless Christian homes, Heather, Denise, Terry, and Shelley came to one of my Bible studies as special guest singers. They were students at Ouachita Baptist University at the time, and I doubt that the word *artists* had ever occurred to them. When they opened their mouths, God opened His heavens, and the rest—as they say—is history.

I was only one of many who got to sit on the sidelines for the years that followed and watch God be huge. I'll never forget how I felt when they accepted their first Dove Award. I wept over the privilege of getting to witness such an amazing work of God from such close proximity.

Foreword

Acts 17:26–27 reads: "From one man He made every nation of men, that they should inhabit the whole earth; and He determined the times set for them and the exact places where they should live. God did this so that men would seek Him and perhaps reach out for Him and find Him, though He is not far from each one of us" (NIV). Whenever I teach these verses, I use Heather, Denise, Terry, and Shelley as the perfect examples of a God who tailor-designs servants for specific generations.

Can you picture Point of Grace in our great-great grandmother's churches? Hardly! *Revival* would have taken on a whole new meaning as much of the congregation would have required CPR. But our generation? I can't think of anyone God has suited more perfectly to minister to His people in our day. I am convinced that some of their greatest works are ahead.

I have celebrated every work Point of Grace has accomplished, but I can honestly say I have never been more excited than I am about *Girls of Grace*. God has given these four young women favor among girls of all ages, and I am thrilled by their determination to be good stewards of their positions of influence.

You are going to love *Girls of Grace*! You're also going to want to grab a copy for every girl you know. This book has the Spirit-empowered capacity to change young lives. It's about time this generation grasped that nothing is cooler than being a Christian.

Ten years ago, as those four college girls sauntered onto that stage, I was quite sure I had never seen a more precious gathering of fresh faces in all my life. Then last night . . . I thought the same thing. Grace lasts. That's all there is to it.

> *A friend loves at all times,*
> *and a brother is born for adversity.*
> Proverbs 17:17 NIV

Introduction

Over the years we have been blessed to meet teenage girls from all across the country—especially during our Girls of Grace seminars. We are so passionate about the content of this book and hope that you will find lots of relevant information to help you with your faith, your family, your friends, yourself, and with boys.

From conversations with many of you, we understand so much more just how hard it is to be a teenage girl in our culture. We pray often for you—that your convictions will be strong and that you will be able to withstand the pressure that often surrounds you. It is our prayer that God will keep you in His care and protect you always. Girls, don't ever forget who you are in Christ and that with the power of the Holy Spirit living in you, you truly can do all things through Christ who strengthens you.

Introduction

So, to all of you precious girls who are looking for answers, this book is our attempt to encourage you in your faith, to challenge you in your walk with Christ, and to aid you in your search for answers to many of life's questions.

In writing this book, we have come to realize more than ever that we do not have all the answers. But we are intimately acquainted with our Mighty God who does hold all the answers. We prayed and studied and sought God's guidance as we wrote the words on the pages of this book.

We ask that you open your hearts as we share what God has placed on our hearts for you. Our hope is that the Lord will use this book to minister to you right where you are. Our prayer for you is that you know you are loved and that the "God of our Lord Jesus Christ, the glorious Father, may give you the Spirit of wisdom and revelation, so that you may know Him better. We pray also that the eyes of your heart may be enlightened in order that you may know the hope to which He has called you, the riches of His glorious inheritance in the saints, and His incomparably great power for us who believe" (Ephesians 1:17–19 NIV).

faith

Dear Point of Grace,

I don't seem to have time for anything anymore. When I first became a Christian, I loved reading my Bible and having a quiet time every day, but with school, track, piano lessons—plus all the chores I'm expected to do—there aren't enough hours in the day for devotionals anymore. And when I'm finally to the point where I have some free time, I just don't feel like reading something so serious. Is it that important to read the Bible every day? I go to church every Sunday and Wednesday. Can't I just learn enough about Jesus and God that way?

What do you think?

Megan

No discipline seems pleasant at the time, but painful. Later on, however, it produces a harvest of righteousness and peace for those who have been trained by it.

Hebrews 12:11 NIV

What's So Good about *Discipline*?

"Have you finished your homework?" "Did you clean your room?" "Don't forget to practice the piano." "Yes, you have to eat all of your peas." Does any of this sound familiar? Well, it sure does to me, and I remember all too clearly my responses as I huffed and puffed and rolled my eyes on my way to do whatever I was told. However, what I thought was a total pain at the time, I now see was for my own good. It was all a lesson in discipline.

By *discipline* I don't mean punishment; I mean training or instruction. That's what my parents were trying to do with all their questions and rules: they were training me, teaching me how to live life responsibly. You see, what we don't understand as teenagers—and what our parents already know—is that much of what we learn as young people will establish who we become as adults. I recently read this story in a book called *Spiritual Disciplines of the Christian Life* by Donald Whitney. He writes:

Imagine six-year-old Kevin, whose parents have enrolled him in music lessons. After school every afternoon, he sits in the living room and reluctantly strums "Home on the Range" while watching his buddies play baseball in the park across the street. That's discipline without direction. It's drudgery.

Now suppose Kevin is visited by an angel one afternoon during guitar practice. In a vision he's taken to Carnegie Hall. He's shown a guitar virtuoso giving a concert. Usually bored by classical music, Kevin is astonished by what he sees and hears. The musician's fingers dance excitedly on the strings with fluidity and grace. Kevin thinks of how stupid and klunky his hands feel when they halt and stumble over the chords. The virtuoso blends clean, soaring notes into a musical aroma that wafts from his guitar. Kevin remembers the toneless, irritating discord that comes stumbling out of his.

But Kevin is enchanted. His head tilts slightly to one side as he listens. He drinks in everything. He never imagined that anyone could play the guitar like this. "What do you think, Kevin?" asks the angel. The answer is a soft, six-year-old's "Wow!" The vision vanishes, and the angel is again standing in front of Kevin in his living room. "Kevin," says the angel, "the wonderful musician you saw is you in a few years." Then pointing at the guitar, the angel declares, "But you must practice!"

I love that story. Now put yourself in Kevin's place. What is the first thing you would do when the angel left? Well, you would practice, of course. Why?

What's So Good about *Discipline*?

Because you would now have a vision of your very own. You would know what you were going to become; you would have a *reason* to be disciplined.

God has a goal in mind for us that is very important to Him. His goal is that we be "conformed to the image of His Son" (Romans 8:29 NASB). But there's a catch. In order for us to make God's goal our own and become like His Son, we must know Jesus intimately. And that takes time and discipline. The primary way we get to know Him is through His Word.

Proverbs 2:6 says: "For the LORD gives wisdom, and from His mouth come knowledge and understanding" (NIV). The Bible is God's inspired Word, and it is the tool He has given us to get to know Him and learn from Him. Second Timothy 3:16–17 says: "All Scripture is God-breathed and is useful for teaching, rebuking, correcting and training in righteousness, so that the man of God may be thoroughly equipped for every good work" (NIV). The more time we spend in His Word, the more we will know Him and His holy character. This is how we begin to fulfill God's goal for us to become like Jesus. If our hearts are in line with God's, we will want to have the same goals for ourselves that He does.

First Timothy 4:7 says: "Discipline yourself for the purpose of godliness" (NASB). The Greek word for "discipline" is *gumnasia,* and you can probably guess what it means. It translates into our English words *gymnasium* or *gymnastics,* and it means "to exercise or discipline." Spending time with God every day is considered spiritual exercise. In order to have a healthy spiritual life, we must discipline—or exercise—ourselves daily in Bible reading and prayer.

Faith—Heather

As a young teenager, I was challenged to begin having a personal devotional or quiet time with God every day. During the first few weeks, it was really hard to make the time. But I was determined, and so every day I would read the Bible, pray, and write in my journal. Before I knew it, my time with God was a regular part of my day. As I finished high school, then college, and now in my adult life, I see my time with God as a *necessity*. Only by spending time with Him am I able to walk in the Spirit and respond to things in a godly way. I thank God that someone made the effort to challenge me in this way. Regular time with God is the most enriching and rewarding experience in my life.

And now I would like to extend the same challenge to you. If you accept this challenge and regularly make time for Him in your life, you will be blessed beyond your dreams. And once you make time with Him a habit, you'll find that if you neglect your quiet time, you will miss Him immensely. The fact of the matter is that you desperately need God. God is the life-giver and the One who nurtures your soul and lavishes His amazing love on you each day. Going about your day without making Him part of it is saying to Him that you don't need Him.

Once, when Jesus was asked which of the commandments was the greatest, he quickly replied: "You shall love the Lord your God with all your heart, and with all your soul, and with all your mind. This is the great and foremost commandment" (Matthew 22:37–38 NASB). Do you love Him like that? If not, wouldn't you like to? You can if you get in the Word. When you love someone, you desire to spend time with him or her. Do you long to spend time with God? When was the last time you read His Word and prayed to Him?

Maybe you *want* to focus on spiritual things but feel stifled because you don't know how to begin. People often tell you that you need to do something yet neglect to teach you *how*. In the next devotional, I'll share some ideas about how to read the Bible and pray every day.

My friend, God delights in you, and His plan is for you to delight in Him. The best time to start is now, and you are on your way!

becoming a girl of grace

STUDY GUIDE

The Relationship

📖 **Opening Scripture:** Ask God to speak to you in a specific way today as you study His Word. Read John 14:6.

Fill in the blanks:* "Jesus answered, 'I am the _____, and the _____ and the _____. No one comes to the Father except through _____.'"

❧ **The Value of Relationship:** Life is made up of relationships. Without them, our lives would be dull and lonely. Think about some of the relationships you have. You have parents, possibly siblings, and friends. Each plays a significant role in your life. You probably can't imagine what life would be like without them.

What's your experience? In what ways have your relationships made your life more meaningful? _____

_____

_____

_____

❧ **The Most Important Relationship of All:** Did you know the Bible teaches there is one relationship that is absolutely critical? It determines the course of your life and your eternal destiny. This relationship is with the Lord Jesus Christ.

 8

The Relationship

What's your experience? Do you have a personal relationship with Jesus Christ?

    ❑ I think so, although I am not 100 percent sure.

    ❑ My parents do, so doesn't that mean I do, too?

    ❑ Yes, I remember when I first invited Him into my life.

    ❑ No, I do not have a relationship with Him, but I want to find out more about how I can.

What does the Word say? According to John 14:6, there is one way to heaven. What is that way? _____

The Bible teaches that the only way a person becomes a Christian is when he or she enters into a relationship with Jesus Christ.

❀ **Myths about What Makes a Christian:** Let's look at some common myths people believe about what makes someone a Christian.

1. If you are "good," you will get into heaven.

What does the Word say? Read Romans 3:23. According to this verse, who is able to be a Christian on her own goodness?

    ❑ Everyone

    ❑ Only those who never commit any of the "big" sins like murder or theft

    ❑ No one. All have sinned and fall short.

    ❑ Nuns are good enough. They can't possibly ever sin.

This passage teaches that every single person has sinned. No one measures up to the holiness of God. No one becomes a Christian on the basis of how good she is.

2. Jesus isn't the only way; all paths and religions lead to heaven.

People who say this often teach that *sincerity* is more important than actual *beliefs*. This may *sound* good, but that doesn't make it right. Let's take some time to think about that statement. If that thinking were true, those who simply believed they were on the right road would end up where they intended, whether or not they took the right road to get there.

You know better than that. You know that there is a difference between *being* on the right road and *believing* you are on the right road when you are really on the wrong one. One will get you where you need to go, and the other will get you lost.

What do you think? Why do you think this myth is so popular?_____

_____

_____

What does the Word say? Read John 14:6 again. According to Jesus, how many roads to heaven are there?

❏ Many
❏ One
❏ Zero
❏ Thousands

3. I am a Christian because my parents are Christians. In the Bible Jesus called individuals to follow Him. Each person had to decide for him- or herself. You also must make the decision as to whether or not you will follow Christ.

4. If I go to church, I am a Christian. Going to church doesn't make you a Christian any more than sitting in your garage will make you a car. Becoming a Christian doesn't have anything to do with the outside things you do. First Samuel 16:7 says, "The Lord does not look at the things man looks at. Man looks at the outward appearance, but the Lord looks at the heart."

❖ What the Bible Says about What Makes a Christian

Fill in the blanks: Read Romans 6:23 and fill in the missing words: "For the _____ of sin is _____, but the _____ is _____ in Christ Jesus our Lord."

This passage teaches that apart from Jesus Christ, we will get what we deserve: death and hell. According to this verse, what is the gift of God? _____

_____

_____

What's your experience? Just as we cannot earn gifts, we cannot earn salvation in Christ. The only way we get a gift is by receiving it. Has there ever been a time when you received the gift of salvation offered in Jesus Christ? If so, describe your experience. _____

_____

_____

What does the Word say? Now read Ephesians 2:8–9. According to this passage, how does one receive eternal life? _____

_____

Why are we told not to boast? _____

_____

_____

Think about it: Jesus came to earth and lived a perfect, sinless life. He then died on the cross to pay for the sins of the world. He died for every sin you ever committed—past, present, and future. On the third day He rose from the dead. He offers forgiveness and eternal life to those who will accept His sacrifice.

Maybe as you are reading this, you realize that you have never personally received Jesus as your Lord and Savior. If you would like to begin a relationship with Jesus, it's time to take the first step and pray the simple prayer below. The words are not magical; rather, they must be the prayer of your heart. Pray this only if you truly mean it.

Jesus, I have never personally accepted Your forgiveness for my sins. Thank You for dying on the cross for me. I realize that when You died,

The Relationship

You paid the price for all of my sins. I receive Your gift of eternal life and invite You into my heart to be my Lord and Savior. Amen.

If you prayed this prayer, make sure you tell a Christian adult. Ask this person to guide you as you continue your new relationship with Jesus.

What does the Word say? Read 2 Corinthians 5:17. What does this passage say about those who have a personal relationship with Christ?

_____

_____

_____

In what ways can you live as the "new creation" that God's Word says you are? _____

_____

_____

✔ **Try This:** If you have been a Christian for a while, remember not everyone has heard this good news. Is there someone with whom you need to share about Jesus? If so, who is it? Write his or her name here. Also write what you will do to share with him or her this week. _____

_____

_____

_____

_____

If you just became a Christian in the course of this study, make sure you keep reading God's Word every day. It will help you grow in your personal relationship with Jesus.

✝ **Living the Word:** Read 2 Corinthians 5:21.

- God made Jesus who had no sin to become *what* on our behalf?
  - ❑ A great leader
  - ❑ Sin
  - ❑ A good friend
  - ❑ A healer

- According to this passage, why did God do this?_____

_____

_____

_____

- What are some things you can do to help yourself grow in righteousness? _____

_____

_____

- What an exchange! Jesus came to earth to take on our sins so that we could take on His righteousness. Thank Him today. _____

_____

The Relationship

_____

_____

_____

_____

_____

_____

_____

Dear Point of Grace,

I know that I should read my Bible every day, but I'm having trouble figuring out where to start. I tried reading it once from beginning to end, but I got confused and overwhelmed with all the details that don't really have anything to do with me. Ever since then, I've thought that I'd get around to starting again, but I never do. I'm really discouraged. What can I do?

Tessa

How can a young person stay pure?
By obeying your word and following its rules.
Psalm 119:9 NLT

The B-i-b-l-e

One of the very first songs I ever learned was "The B-i-b-l-e." Remember that song? "The B-i-b-l-e, yes, that's the book for me. I stand alone on the Word of God, the B-i-b-l-e." I love that song. As a matter of fact, I've heard Denise's son Spence sing it a few times, and I must say that every time I hear it, it brings back memories of going to vacation Bible school and Sunday school.

I'll never forget the day I got my first Bible. It was white and had beautifully colored pictures in it. I felt very grown up when I carried it to church for the first time. I grew up knowing that the Bible was God's Word and that it was a very important book. Now that I am older, and maybe even a little wiser, I see that reading the Bible is not just important—it is vital to the Christian walk.

I heard my husband say recently that the Bible is God's thoughts to us.

17

I like that idea. In addition to giving us insight into how God *thinks*, the Bible is the primary way that God *speaks* to us. His Word teaches us how to live a life that pleases Him and glorifies His name. Second Peter 1:3 says that "as we know Jesus better, His divine power gives us everything we need for living a godly life" (NLT). The way we get to "know Jesus better" is by reading and studying the Bible.

You know, it's not easy to live life the way God wants us to. How can you stand up against the temptations and difficulties of this life? How can you be the friend God calls you to be? How can you be an obedient daughter and a kind sister? How can you behave purely and righteously when you're out with a guy you really like and don't want to lose? God knows that you face these difficult questions. The writer of Psalm 119 asks the very same kind of question—and he gives you the answer: "How can a young person stay pure? By obeying your word and following its rules" (verse 9 NLT). You can't very well obey God's Word and follow its rules if you don't know what it says. Spending time in His Word is a key ingredient to keeping yourself pure.

You may be thinking, *I'm only a teenager. What's the rush? I'll make time for it when I'm older.* Let me tell you a story that will demonstrate why it's so important to start now. Not long ago, my husband and I and a friend of ours were out making random door-to-door visits. (We're part of a Tuesday-night evangelism/visitation group.) We ended up visiting with two young men who were college students. The first young man graciously invited us in. As we sat down, I was horrified to see a pornographic magazine sitting right on top of the coffee table. We began to ask him questions about his life, and it saddened me deeply to find out that he was raised in church. He knew all the right answers to our questions about what it took to go to heaven, but he pretty much admitted that he was a party animal. He said that he'd never been into reading the Bible but that if he ever started feeling bad about how he was living, he would pick it up. My husband, Brian, was very bold in his response to him but also very kind. As we left, my heart was aching, and I couldn't say a word as we walked to our next house.

The young man at this house also invited us in, and lo and behold, sitting right there on the coffee table was yet another pornographic magazine. I was thankful that he removed the magazine as we sat down to visit with him. Like the first young man, he also told us that he had grown up in church, and he, too, answered all of our questions correctly. He also knew that he wasn't living right. But this guy was different; it was obvious that he was miserable in his sin. We prayed with him and invited him to the college service at our church and asked him if there was anything that we could do for him. He told us that he wasn't very familiar with the Bible and asked if we could give him some scriptures to read—which, of course, Brian did.

Now, what do you see in this scenario? Both of these young men were raised in the church, yet neither had ever established a habit of reading their Bibles regularly. However, they both recognized the Bible as the book to go to when they felt bad about their lifestyles.

Here is what I see, my friend. It is not enough to go to church. One sermon on Sunday, no matter how good it is, will not supply you with the strength you need for every day of the week. I don't know about you, but I need God daily. I need Him every second of every minute.

In 2 Timothy 3 the apostle Paul writes to his young friend and disciple Timothy and tells him: "Remain faithful to the things you have been taught. You know they are true, for you know you can trust those who taught you. You have been taught the holy Scriptures from childhood, and they have given you the wisdom to receive the salvation that comes by trusting in Christ Jesus" (verses 14–15 NLT). We see from this passage that Timothy began learning from the Word of God when he was a child. Then in verses 16 and 17, Paul tells Timothy why spending time with God's Word is so important: "All Scripture is inspired by God and profitable for *teaching*, for *reproof*, for *correction*, for *training* in righteousness; so that the man of God may be adequate, equipped for every good work" (NASB). I like what Warren Wiersbe says in his commentary on verse 16. He says that we need *teaching* to learn what *is* right, we need *reproof* to learn what is *not* right, we need *correction* to learn how to *be* right, and we need *training* in righteousness to learn how to *stay* right.

This passage is the summation of why we need the Bible and why it is essential for our growth as godly young women.

Now, I promised you in the last devotional that I'd try to do more than just tell you *what* to do and actually tell you *how* to do it. Well, here are a few different ideas to get you started in your daily Bible reading.

Daily devotional books. There are numerous daily devotional books out there. When I first started having a quiet time, I used one called *Our Daily*

Bread. It had a Scripture reading every day and then a devotional thought based on the passage that you read. Devotional books can be very helpful; just be careful not to depend more on what the devotional writer says than what the Bible says.

The Book of Proverbs. You may know this already, but there are thirty-one chapters in the Book of Proverbs—one for each day of the month. I have read a chapter a day for years. When you finish, you can start right over again. Honestly, it never gets old.

The Book of Psalms. The Book of Psalms has 150 chapters. You can read a psalm a day for five months. I love reading the psalms.

The whole Bible. I challenge you to set the goal of reading the Bible all the way through. It may sound overwhelming, but you can take your time. It takes a while, and there are some difficult passages, but it is altogether a wonderful experience. You might try an easy-to-read version like the New Living Translation. This translation is more accurate than a "paraphrase," and it's easier to read than some of the other versions.

The "how" of reading the Bible every day can be different for everyone. You'll find that the more you read the Bible on a daily basis, the more you will work out your own system of doing it. What is important is that you do it and that you do it consistently.

In Isaiah 55 God speaks beautifully about His Word. I love this passage: "The rain and snow come down from the heavens and stay on the ground to water the earth. They cause the grain to grow, producing seed for the farmer and bread for the hungry. It is the same with my word. I send it out, and it always produces fruit. It will accomplish all I want it to, and it will prosper everywhere I send it" (verses 10–11 NLT).

What does this mean? It means that God, through His Word, gives us all we need. He nourishes us, He gives us strength, and He equips us to live a godly life and minister the good news of the gospel of Jesus Christ to others.

My friend, reading God's Word and spending time with Him consistently are the most important parts of becoming a godly young woman. I pray that you will make them consistent parts of your life. And I promise that, if you do, you will be richly rewarded.

STUDY
GUIDE

The Time of Your Life

📖 **Opening Scripture:** Ask God to teach you His truth today as you study His Word. Read Psalm 27:4.

❁ **"One Thing"**

Fill in the blanks: Reread Psalm 27:4 and fill in the missing words. "_____ thing I _____ of the LORD, this is what I _____: that I may dwell in the house of the LORD _____ the days of my life, to gaze upon the beauty of the LORD and to seek him in his temple."

What do you think? If you could only ask for one thing from the Lord, what would it be? _____

_____

The psalmist shows his answer in the verse above. What is the one thing he asks of the Lord?_____

_____

Is this your heart's prayer as well? Why or why not? _____

_____

_____

❁ **Seek More Than Your Personal Needs:** Think about the last time you asked God for something. Maybe your list was filled with requests for things, but you never asked God to reveal more of

Himself to you. It isn't wrong to ask God to meet our needs; as a matter of fact, we are commanded to do this. However, we must remember that the most important thing we can ask for is more intimacy with God.

Think about it: Imagine that you had a friend who constantly came to you asking for things she wanted or needed. You would listen and try to help, but what if her needs were all she ever talked about? What would that tell you about the importance your friend places on *you?* _____

_____

_____

_____

We often do this very thing to God. We rush into His presence with our needs without ever taking time to listen to Him through His Word. Why do you think we do this? _____

_____

_____

_____

❧ **Too Busy for the Best?** Many of us don't think we can fit spending time with God into our schedules. After all, we have busy lives. We have responsibilities and activities that demand our time and energy. It is so hard to fit everything in.

Faith—Study Guide

What's your experience? Look back over the last week. Does the way you spent your time reflect a desire to grow in your relationship with God? Why or why not? _____

_____

_____

_____

_____

What does the Word say? Reread Psalm 27:4. In the Psalms, many times the author's name is listed above the psalm he wrote. If your Bible lists the author, write his name in the space provided. _____

_____

Read Psalm 27:1–3. What insight into David's life do these scriptures provide?

- ❏ He lived in Bible times, so he wasn't busy at all.
- ❏ His life was filled with stress and difficulty, but he chose to prioritize his time with God.
- ❏ He didn't write this psalm.
- ❏ He spent very little time with God.

What words in Psalm 27:4 show us that David prized his relationship with God? _____

_____

_____

✿ Time to Worship

What do you think? What is meant by the phrase "gaze upon the beauty of the Lord"?

- ❑ To literally see God
- ❑ To spend time with Him in worship and study of His Word
- ❑ To go to church
- ❑ To be holy

What's your experience? David spent time with God, worshiping Him and learning about His character. Do you set apart time each day to do this?

- ❑ I do it when I am not busy.
- ❑ No, I don't, but I am willing to learn more about it.
- ❑ Yes, but I need to grow in consistency.
- ❑ Yes. I am not perfect, but I try to spend time with God each day.

✿ Time Alone with God: If you want to grow in your relationship with God, you must spend time alone with Him each day. This time with Him is often referred to as a quiet time. It is a time you set aside to pray and read God's Word.

In Psalm 119:33–35, the writer makes three requests of God. As you spend time with God, He will do three things in *your* life as well:

Faith—Study Guide

1. He will teach you His Word and His ways. Why is it so important to know God's Word? _____

_____

2. He will give you understanding. In which areas of life do *you* need more understanding?_____

_____

_____

3. He will direct you. One of the best ways to understand His plan for your life is by seeking Him through His Word. Has there been a time when you found a passage of Scripture that guided you in a decision you had to make? If so, describe that experience. _____

_____

_____

_____

_____

❁ **Making It Happen:** Just as any habit develops over time, so does the discipline of a quiet time. You probably don't forget to leave your house without brushing your teeth, do you? Well, after you develop the habit of a quiet time, it will come as naturally as brushing your teeth.

There are four things you need to consider before beginning your quiet time:

The Time of Your Life

1. When? Determine what time of day you will have your quiet time. Will it be in the morning or the evening? Many people decide that morning works best so they can meet with God before starting the day.

2. What? In order to get the most out of your time with God, plan what you will do. There are many devotional books in Christian bookstores that can be of help. Make sure that whatever else you do, you spend time in God's Word. You can do this by reading one chapter from the book of Proverbs a day or one psalm a day. You can read the whole Bible through, a few chapters a day, in an easy-to-understand translation like the New International Version or the New Living Translation. Many people write down what God taught them in a journal. It doesn't need to be a long entry, just something that reminds you of what you learned that day.

3. Where? Pick a special place to have your quiet time where you can be alone and uninterrupted. It is probably not a good idea to have your quiet time in bed for reasons you probably know well. You may find yourself facedown on your Bible.

4. How? Begin by asking God to speak to you. Next, spend some time in prayer, confessing any known sins to God and making requests for what you need. Read a passage out of His Word and think about how you can apply it to your life. Is there a command, a promise, or a warning? Write down what God has shown you so that you can look back on it and remember. Just as our interactions with others vary from day to day, so will our time with God. Don't get so "stuck" in the routine that you miss out on hearing from Him. The key is to be disciplined yet flexible.

✿ **The Blessings of Discipline:** Discipline simply means making wise choices about how we spend our time. We don't have to drop out of all of our activities; we simply must put the most important things first.

As you start this habit, make sure you set realistic goals. If you miss one day, don't quit altogether; just start back the next day. Don't be surprised to find that eventually a short quiet time won't be enough to satisfy you as you fall more in love with Jesus.

Fill in the blanks: Read Hebrews 12:11 and fill in the missing words: "No discipline seems _____ at the time, but painful. Later on, however, it produces a harvest of _____ and _____ for those who have been trained by it."

What does the Word say? What two benefits of discipline are listed in the passage?_____

✔ **Try This:** In order to have a quiet time each day, you may need to reprioritize some activities. You may decide to get up fifteen minutes earlier or give up a favorite TV show. Write the actions you will take this week to prioritize having a quiet time. _____

_____

✝ **Living the Word:** Read Psalm 143:8.

• This verse is a prayer to God. Will you make it your prayer today?
If so, write it down and spend some time thinking about what it
means. Next, offer it up to Him as your prayer._____

_____

_____

_____

_____

_____

_____

Dear Point of Grace,

When I first became a Christian, I couldn't wait to have quiet time with God. Now I find myself going hours, even days without really praying. I try to pray, but my mind drifts to other things. I'm beginning to feel like I don't even know how to pray!

Please help!

Laura

For God did not give us a spirit of timidity,
but a spirit of power, of love and of self-discipline.
2 Timothy 1:7 NIV

What's a "Spiritual Discipline"?

Have you ever heard anyone talk about "spiritual disciplines" and wondered what on earth they were talking about? No, it doesn't mean some kind of *cosmic punishment*. Far from it. Spiritual disciplines are habits that we practice regularly to help us grow spiritually. They include habits like meditating on (thinking about) God's Word, reading and studying your Bible, and spending quiet alone-time with God. There are many spiritual disciplines that help us live the abundant Christian life, but I want to concentrate on three that have been an important part of deepening my walk with God—*praying, journaling,* and *memorizing Scripture.* These three practices, more than anything else, have enhanced my relationship with God.

Prayer. One summer at youth camp, a friend of mine wrote in my Bible "JE-333: God's phone number." Now, honestly, at first I had no idea what that meant, but I finally realized that he wrote it in the margin of Jeremiah 33:3, which says, "Call to Me, and I will answer you, and I will tell you great and mighty things, which you do not know" (NASB). Now, I don't know that I would use the "God's phone number" thing, but the point of the verse is prayer, and I always want to use that.

Now, when I talk about prayer, I'm talking about more than the prayers you pray with other people listening in. In Matthew 6:6 Jesus says, "When you pray, go away by yourself, shut the door behind you, and pray to your Father secretly. Then your Father, who knows all secrets, will reward you" (NLT). I gather from this verse that prayer is personal and private and that it's important to get alone with God. Of course I pray publicly and with my husband and intimate friends and family, but my deepest prayer life is a "closet" thing.

And prayer is more than asking God for things—even when we're asking for other people. Prayer is also about getting to know God. In the book *Becoming a Woman of Prayer,* Cynthia Heald wrote: "Often my prayer is for God to show me how to please Him. I think in terms of active doing with people, but God receives pleasure from our wanting to be with Him." Can you identify with Cynthia? I can. I, too, sometimes get all wrapped up in doing things for and with *people,* when God wants me to spend time with *Him.*

I love what Oswald Chambers said about prayer in his devotional *My Utmost for His Highest:* "When a man is born from above, the life of the Son of God is born in him, and he can either starve that life or nourish it. Prayer is the way the life of God is nourished. We look upon prayer as a means of getting things for ourselves; the Bible's idea of prayer is that we may get to know God Himself." Some days, I have a hard time getting started in my prayer—I just can't find the words. Perhaps God is encouraging me to nourish the "life of the Son of God" in me. Maybe He just wants me to be still and get to know Him. We were created for fellowship with God, and prayer is a beautiful way to have that fellowship with Him.

Okay, now that we've talked a little about what prayer is, let me share with you a couple of "how-tos." The first is a formula I learned when I was growing up. You may already know it: It's based on the word *ACTS*.

- *A is for adoration*, which is praising God and telling Him how truly awesome He is and how much you love Him.
- *C is for confession*. When you confess your sins to God, be as specific as you possibly can. If you do this, you'll start seeing what you repeatedly confess, and you'll be more aware of your weaknesses and better able to ask for God's help. And make sure that you not only confess but also repent of, or turn away from, your sin.
- *T is for thanksgiving*. Thank the Lord for all the many blessings that He gives you daily. Again, be specific, because not only does it bless God's heart, it opens your eyes to how great He is.
- *S is for supplication*. Supplication is humbly asking God to help you with your personal needs and the needs of others.

Another very powerful way to pray is to pray Scripture. What could be more powerful than praying God's inspired Word back to the One who inspired it?

Here's an example based on Psalm 27:1, which says, "The LORD is my light and my salvation—so why should I be afraid? The LORD protects me from danger—so why should I tremble?" (NLT). Here's how you can pray this back to God:

Lord, you are my light, and light does away with darkness. You light my path and make things clear. You are my salvation; You have saved me from my sin. You are my protector from all danger. So, Lord, I have no reason to fear, because You have promised that You will never leave me or forsake me. I am so grateful that you came into my heart and made me whole and secure and safe. I am so thankful that you are there.

Praying God's Word is not hard, and it is very rewarding. I'd like to recommend two books that can help you learn to pray the Scripture: Donald Whitney's book *Spiritual Disciplines for the Christian Life* and Beth Moore's book *Praying God's Word*. Now let's look at another spiritual discipline.

Journaling. When I talk about journaling, I'm really talking about a specific way of praying. I have been journaling since I was in junior high, except back then I called it writing in my diary. There is something very freeing about writing your thoughts to God. When I journal, I tell God my thoughts and dreams and fears and successes. Oh, I know that He already knows these things, but it has always been good for me to write them out. Some days I may write one sentence, and on other days I may take up several pages, writing from the very depth of my soul.

Only God knows what is in the pages of my journals. When I think about journaling, I often think about the psalmist David and how so many of his psalms sound like journal entries written to the Lord. David writes about his struggles and about his times of rejoicing. I can identify with much of what he writes. I bet you can, too.

If you had asked me ten years ago if I would ever share something I had written in my journal, I would have said "No way!" However, when I was preparing to write this devotional, I spent time reading through some of my old journals, and it was such a wonderful experience that I thought I would share an entry with you.

Tuesday, October 13, 1992. Bless the Lord, O my soul. All that is within me, bless His Holy name. Oh, Lord, You are so faithful. Thank You for revealing and teaching me that nothing is impossible with You. The key is "with You." I need Your presence in every second of every day.

As you know, Lord, there are days that my heart is discontent. I pray that You will help me learn from Moses and the children of Israel that, even when my circumstances are bleak and I think I can't go on, You are with me. You are my provider, and it does not please You when I complain.

Lord, I know that You meet my every need, but sometimes I doubt because You don't meet my need the way I think You should; but no matter what, You are faithful to care for me. Forgive me for my moments of discontent and doubt. I will count my trials as joy, and I will not lose heart at doing good. And, Father, with Your strength, I will not grow weary.

Lord, carry me through this day and help me glorify You in all that I say and do. Thank you for Your everlasting, unchanging love.

Faith—Heather

Reading back through my journal, I am amazed at how much I've changed through the years. My life has been a bit of a roller coaster, and most of those ups and downs are written in the pages of my journals. The thing that leaves me awestruck is that the one thing that never changed in all my years of journal entries is the presence of God. He was and is always there, and as I read through the pages of my life, I was so encouraged to see His faithfulness.

Today, I want to encourage you to begin journaling. I promise that when you look back years later, you, too, will be amazed at how actively involved God is in your life.

Scripture memorization. Finally, a truly vital spiritual discipline is memorizing Scripture. Doing this will help you grow in intimacy with God and will help you be more effective in living out His will for your life. Most of you have probably memorized a verse here and there, but have you ever memorized an entire psalm or a long passage of Scripture? I have to be honest with you: It wasn't until I married Brian that I began to memorize more than one verse of Scripture.

Before I was challenged by Brian, I had always claimed that I didn't have a very good memory. But I finally figured out that when it comes to things I love, like movie actors and fashion and music, I remember just fine. This realization convinced me, and I started memorizing passages of Scripture. It is amazing how the passages I commit to memory pop up in my mind just when I need them. Whether I am being tempted or am presented with a ministry opportunity, God's words are much more powerful than my own.

What's a "Spiritual Discipline"?

Psalm 119:11 says, "I have hidden your word in my heart, that I might not sin against you" (NIV). Just think how much of God's Word will live in you when you are an adult if you'll start memorizing Scripture now.

Let me share some tactics that have helped me in this discipline.

- Write the verses you are memorizing on Post-it notes, and stick them in several places where you will see them during the day.
- Write your memory verses in your journal. It always helps to write them down.
- Find a friend who will memorize along with you and keep you accountable. You could even offer each other incentives like saying that whoever finishes last has to treat the other to a meal.
- Say the verses over and over in your mind right before you go to bed. While you sleep, you may unconsciously think about these verses because that was the last thing you thought about before you went to bed. And who knows—it might even be the first thing you think about in the morning.

The neat thing about all three of these disciplines is how they work together. You can write your prayers to God and the verses you want to memorize in your journal. Then you can use the verses that you've memorized to pray God's Word in your personal prayer time.

My heart's desire is that you find the joy in these spiritual disciplines that I have. I pray for you what the apostle Paul prayed for the Christians in the city of Ephesus: I ask "God, the glorious Father of our Lord Jesus Christ, to give you spiritual wisdom and understanding, so that you might grow in your knowledge of God. I pray that your hearts will be flooded with light so that you can understand the wonderful future he has promised to those he called. I want you to realize what a rich and glorious inheritance he has given to his people. I pray that you will begin to understand the incredible greatness of his power for us who believe him" (Ephesians 1:17–19 NLT).

STUDY GUIDE

What Is Your Focus?

📖 **Opening Scripture:** Ask God to speak to you in a powerful way today. Next, read Ephesians 5:8–10.

❀ **Finding Your Purpose:** Have you ever determined the purpose for your life? I am not talking about the details such as what kind of career you'll have or where you want to live someday. Rather, what is the overall goal of your life? This may seem like a huge question to be thinking about at such a young age, but the answer will determine the whole course of your life. Purpose is like a compass. Without it, you will wander aimlessly.

What do you think? How will your purpose help you make choices that reflect the light of Jesus within you? _____

_____

What does the Word say? Our purpose should be set by who we are. According to Ephesians 5:8–10, what is your identity if you are a Christian? _____

How should that affect your daily life?_____

_____

Fill in the blanks: Read Ephesians 5:9 and fill in the missing words: "For the fruit of the light consists in all _____, _____ and _____."

 42

What Is Your Focus?

What does the Word say? What are some ways you can obey the command in verse 10 to "find out what pleases the Lord"?

- ❏ Ask Him to show me out of His Word.
- ❏ Wait for Him to verbally tell me.
- ❏ Just try to figure it out for myself.
- ❏ Do what others do and hope that works.

Think about it: Do you ever wonder what God's will is for your life? God's Word is the best place to find out His will. He doesn't hold out on us; we are simply not diligent in knowing His Word.

What does the Word say? Read 2 Corinthians 5:14–15. According to verse 14, what is our motivation for living?

- ❏ His judgment
- ❏ Reward
- ❏ Knowing it is the right thing to do
- ❏ His love

Jesus' love compels us to no longer live for ourselves. We must consider ourselves dead to our own sinful desires and live to please Him.

According to verse 15, what should be our purpose for living?_____

_____

_____

Faith—Study Guide

❁ **Our "Calling":** Christians are called to glorify Christ in all we do. The word *glorify* simply means that we honor and draw attention to God. This doesn't mean that we need to check into a monastery; rather, we are to glorify God in our everyday lives. If we are studying, playing sports, or just going about our daily activities, God calls us to live in such a way that we honor Him.

Think about it: Think about an average day in your life. List the activities you participate in and the places you go. _____

_____

_____

_____

_____

_____

Now write one way you can glorify God as you do each thing on your list. _____

_____

_____

_____

_____

Are there things you participate in that do not glorify God? If so, will you surrender those areas to Him today? _____

What action steps will you take to remove these behaviors from your life? _____

What Is Your Focus?

_____

_____

_____

_____

✿ **Focus Your Heart:** The key to glorifying God in our daily lives is focus. Did you know that whatever you focus on is what you glorify?

What's your experience? What do you focus your heart and mind on each day? _____

_____

_____

Fill in the blanks: Read Hebrews 12:2. Fill in the missing words: "Let us _____ our eyes on _____, the author and perfecter of our faith, who for the joy set before him endured the _____, scorning its shame, and sat down at the _____ _____ of the _____ of God."

What does the Word say? According to this passage, what should be our constant focus? _____

What's your experience? If you deliberately focused on Jesus tomorrow, what would your day be like? _____

_____

_____

Faith—Study Guide

✔ **Try This:** You may want to place Scripture verses in your locker or your schoolbooks. Maybe you will memorize a different Scripture verse each week. There are many things you can do to help you focus on Him. Be as creative as you can, and write some practical things you will do to help you remember to focus on Jesus each day.

_____

_____

_____

✟ **Living the Word:** Read 2 Corinthians 5:9.

• According to the writer, what is his goal? _____

_____

• Are you willing to make this your life goal as well? Why or why not? _____

_____

_____

_____

• Is there something you need to change in order to make this verse true in your life? If so, what steps will you take this week to make that change? _____

_____

_____

_____

What Is Your Focus?

• Did you know that pleasing God on the earth prepares us to glorify Him for all eternity? Will you purpose to start now? How will trying to please God affect what you do and say in the coming weeks? _____

_____

_____

_____

_____

beauty tips

✿ Getting plenty of sleep can keep your skin looking fresh—at least eight hours a night is a good rule of thumb.

✿ If you're on a tight budget, check out your local beauty school for supercheap manicures and pedicures. It's much less expensive than a regular salon and can be lots more fun than a movie!

✿ For supersoft feet, try scrubbing them with an inexpensive, grainy exfoliant, then slathering them with tons of Vaseline and sleeping with socks over the Vaseline. In the morning you won't believe how soft your feet are.

✿ Never sleep in your makeup. Try taking it off right when you get home from school and putting on a light moisturizer. That way, if you're really tired, it will already be done come bedtime!

❀ Do something completely for the benefit of someone else. Volunteering is a great way to meet new people, become a more grateful person, and make someone happy all at the same time. Try calling your local hospital, nursing home, or women's shelter to sign up for volunteer services.

❀ Use the times you're alone to talk to God about the stuff that's important to you. When you're driving or riding in the car or doing the dishes are great times to tell Him what's up with you.

❀ Make a conscious effort every day to think before you speak and to keep your unkind words to yourself. Ask God every morning to help you.

❀ Are you at odds with anyone? Use today to make peace. Don't be afraid to apologize or accept the blame for something. The ability to admit faults is a mark of inner beauty.

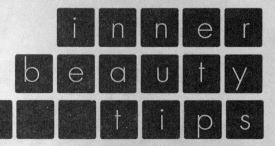

inner beauty tips

family

Dear Point of Grace,

My parents are driving me crazy! They are so strict and so out of it! They don't let me hang out in the places most of my friends are allowed to go to. They insist on knowing where I'm going, who I'm going with, and what I'm doing every second of the day. And then I have to call them if my plans change or if I'm going to be late. And all of this leads to fights—lots of them. I don't remember a weekend in the last year when we didn't end up yelling at each other. I want a better relationship with my parents, but they just don't get it! Can you help?

Natalia

Honor your father and your mother,
so that you may live long in the land
the LORD your God is giving you.
Exodus 20:12 NIV

Honor Your Father and Mother

I wish I could say that I followed the advice I'm about to give you, but the fact of the matter is—I didn't. Don't get me wrong; I wasn't a bad teenager. I didn't drink or do drugs, but I did have a famously smart mouth.

I probably didn't fight with my mom and dad any more or any less than the average teenage girl, but now it occurs to me that God doesn't call us to be average teenagers but to live our lives by a higher standard. (My mom's probably thinking, *Too bad that didn't occur to you when you were thirteen, smarty-pants.*) Ephesians 5:1–2 talks of this higher standard—the notion of modeling our actions after Christ. It says "Be *imitators* of God, therefore, as dearly loved children and live a life of love, just as Christ loved us and gave himself up for us" (NIV). Hmm…"imitators of God." That concept will change the way you react to your parents real quick—if you really take it to heart.

I'm here to tell you that following two simple concepts will instantly strengthen your relationship with your mom and dad and, more important, will please your heavenly parent—God. Now, I don't use the word *simple* as in "easy," but *simple* as in "basic and foundational." These two concepts are *honor* and *obedience*.

So what does honor mean, anyway? In the context of Exodus 20:12, "Honor your father and mother" means to hold them in high esteem and respect. And by obedience, I mean being a big enough person to accept what your parents say and obey them whether you agree or not. (Ugh! That's a hard one!)

I totally understand that it's hard to honor your parents when you want to do something they don't want you to do. Can I tell you how uncool I felt when I wasn't allowed to go to 8 Wheels on Friday nights as a teenager? "What is 8 Wheels?" you might ask. Well, it was only the *only* place to be on Friday nights when I was in the seventh grade. As much as I wanted to be with the kids I perceived to be the coolest seventh-graders in town, my parents wouldn't let me. They didn't think a seventh-grade girl should be dropped off by herself at a roller-skating rink where older kids were hanging out and you could come and go as you please. Honestly, looking back, I can see they were right. It was a rather "seedy" place, but I didn't see it that way then. See? I had different eyes then.

Then, in the eighth grade, the "cool" people moved on to Star Systems. Now *that* was the ultimate place to be. It was *much* cooler than 8 Wheels. It was a dark video arcade in an outdoor strip mall, and it was completely unsupervised. Let's just say, some "not so great stuff" went on outside that arcade. As my luck would have it, just about the time that 8 Wheels was out and Star Systems was in, Mom and Dad said I could go to the roller rink, but then it was too late—it just wasn't cool anymore. My friends had "moved on."

I remember what seemed like endless Friday nights, crying to my parents, pleading with them to let me go where my friends were going—yelling, smarting off, or whatever I thought would convince them to let me go. Of course, none of my tactics worked. Now I understand that it wasn't necessarily *me* they didn't trust, but simply the potential dangers of the situations. In reality, they were protecting me.

You're probably thinking, *8 Wheels? Star Systems? How completely ridiculous and insignificant. How completely lame!* This, my sweet friend, is *exactly* my point! What then seemed like the hugest deal in the world is absolutely meaningless now. If I had taken the time to step back and look at the situation realistically, it would have changed the way I reacted. How much better would it have been if I'd simply obeyed my parents? That's right, honor and obey—maybe even cheerfully. Obedience and respect actually bring better long-term results than do whining and fighting. That kind of maturity can actually make your parents trust and respect you more.

This may sound a little cheesy, but if my attitude had been different, I might have even enjoyed some awesome Friday nights, making memories and having some quality family time with good ol' Mom and Dad.

In reality, obedience is our *only* option. It's not like God gives us another choice. Ephesians 6:1 says, "Children, obey your parents in the Lord, for this is right" (NIV). It doesn't say, "Children, obey your parents when it's easy," or,

"Children, obey your parents if you agree with them." It pretty much just says, "Obey."

This may seem so cut and dry—unreasonable almost—but we need to understand that God didn't give us these commands to make our teenage years miserable. Actually, His intent is just the opposite. God is interested in protecting us just as much or more than our parents are. He absolutely loves and adores us. We are His *children*, and He loves us as only a perfect Father can.

So, even when it's really hard and we don't understand, we have to trust God and obey Him. And even when we don't agree, if we love Him, we will keep His commandments. First John 5:3 says, "This is love for God: to obey his commands"—and one of the most important commands is that we "honor our father and mother" (NIV).

Now that I've lived a little more of life, I can see clearly how smart my parents really were. Trust me . . . I never thought I would say that—not in a million years. But it's true. I will probably never know the trouble they kept me out of just by saying no. Too bad I had to give them such a hard time about it.

Life is not about getting our way, but about pleasing God and doing things His way, and it's about being mature enough to handle it when we don't get to do exactly as we please.

So . . . in the situations that seem like a huge deal and in the little everyday things of life, our parents deserve our respect and obedience, simply because they are our parents. As a young woman trying to follow Christ and imitate Him, honoring and obeying your mom and dad are some of the most important fundamental things you can do to show your love for Him.

Parents: God's Design?

📖 **Opening Scripture:** Ask God to speak to you today as you study His Word. Then read Ephesians 6:1–3.

❀ **Authority That Protects:** Imagine a world with no rules, no authority figures, and no restrictions. Although some may think this sounds like freedom, others recognize it for what it truly is: chaos. God provides authorities to protect us. Without authority, our world would be a mess. There would be no rules or laws, no regulations, and no personal rights. God has graciously provided authority to be the umbrella that protects us from harmful consequences.

Did you know that the Bible teaches that parents are God's design for authority in your life? This may not seem like good news to you now, but when you see it from God's perspective, you will realize that it is great news.

Think about it: List one way that a God-given authority protects you.

_____

_____

❀ **Honor Your Father and Mother**

Fill in the blanks: Fill in the missing words from Ephesians 6:2:
"_____ your father and mother—which is the first commandment with a _____."

Parents: God's Design?

What does the Word say? Read Exodus 20:12. What does God promise to the one who honors her father and mother?

❑ She will have riches and fame.

❑ She will never get grounded.

❑ She will live long in the land God promised.

❑ She will have the peace that passes understanding.

What do you think? The promise in Exodus is listed as one of the Ten Commandments. Knowing this, what level of importance does God place on honoring your parents? _____

_____

_____

God promises that those who obey will have a full life. This refers not only to *quantity* of days but also to *quality* of days. Why do you think the relationship with our parents is critical to having a full life?

_____

_____

❧ **What It Means to "Honor" Your Parents:** Ephesians 6:2 calls us to honor our parents. Look up the word *honor* in a dictionary and write down what you find. _____

_____

_____

_____

Family—Study Guide

Think about it: Part of honoring your parents is shown in how you communicate with them. Does the way you talk to your parents show that you respect them? Do you listen to them, or do you argue and talk back? How about your body language? Sometimes we say more with our facial expressions than we ever do with our lips. When you speak about your parents, do you show respect for them? On a scale of 1 to 10 (10 being the best), rate how your speech to and about your parents measures up to God's standard: _____

What does the Word say? Read Proverbs 4:1–4, 10–12. The true test of whether someone honors her parents is if she obeys them.

Obedience is crucial because it reveals our hearts. Although obedience is often not the easiest choice, it is always the best one. Recall a time when you obeyed your parents and were glad, even though it wasn't the easiest choice to make. _____

_____

_____

_____

✿ Why Should You Obey Your Parents? Obedience has lifelong rewards.

Fill in the blank: Reread Proverbs 4:10 and fill in the missing words: "Listen, my son, accept what I say, and the years of your life

_____."

Parents: God's Design?

What's your experience? Has there been a time when obeying your parents has literally saved your life? Take some time to think about your answer and then record it in the blanks. _____

_____

_____

_____

What does the Word say? Reread Proverbs 4:10–12. According to this passage, what are the benefits of obeying your parents? _____

_____

_____

_____

Think about it: Even though this passage promises a benefit, the main reason we obey our parents is because the Lord commands it.

Ephesians 6:1 says, "Obey your parents...for this is right." When we obey our parents, we are also obeying the Lord. Likewise, when we disobey our parents, we are disobeying God.

❧ Authority Was God's Idea

What does the Word say? Read Romans 13:1–2. According to verse 1, who established authority? _____

Knowing this, how will you treat those in positions over you, such as your parents? _____

_____

According to the passage, what happens when people rebel against their authorities?_____

_____

_____

Who brings judgment on them?_____

What do you think? What are some ways judgment comes when we disobey?_____

_____

_____

_____

Think about it: To disobey your parents is to disregard God's commands and His ultimate authority over our lives. The only time it is okay to disobey your authorities is when they ask you to violate a principle from God's Word. This is a rare instance, but if this does happen, talk with an older and wiser leader for advice on how to handle the situation.

❧ Putting Obedience into Practice

Think about it: Are there specific steps of obedience God is calling you to take? Maybe you need to go to your parents and confess your disobedience. If so, make it a point to do that today.

What action or attitude is God leading you to change in order to honor your parents? _____

Parents: God's Design?

_____
_____
_____
_____

You may be thinking, *I would obey, but my parents make mistakes.* All parents make mistakes because they are human, just like you are. This doesn't lessen your responsibility to obey. God calls you to love and respect them anyway.

Pray about it: If respecting your parents is difficult for you, you may want to start praying for them each day. Ask God to help you see them through His eyes. Pray that He will give them wisdom and you a heart to obey.

✔ **Try This:** Make a list of the authorities God has placed over you. Don't forget to list your parents and, if you have them, stepparents. Keep in mind your roles as student, church member, and citizen of your town and nation. Beside each name write down one way you can honor each authority. _____

_____
_____
_____
_____
_____

Family—Study Guide

✝ **Living the Word:** Read Colossians 3:22–25. You may have noticed that this passage addresses the readers as "slaves." This simply means it applies to anyone who is under the authority of another person. For this reason, it applies to everyone.

• Why is it harder to obey when we know no one else is looking?

_____

_____

_____

_____

• Why is it so important to obey when people aren't watching, as well as when they are? _____

_____

_____

_____

• How can you apply verse 23 to the responsibilities you have at home? _____

_____

_____

_____

• How should this passage change the way you treat your parents?

_____

_____

_____

Parents: God's Design?

_____

_____

_____

• What action steps will you take this week to make sure you honor your parents? _____

_____

_____

_____

_____

_____

Dear Point of Grace,

My little sister is making me nuts! She's five years younger than I am, and we have absolutely nothing in common, but she insists on following me around everywhere I go.

The worst is when my friends are over. She's constantly knocking on my bedroom door with some excuse for coming in. My friends and I have things we want to talk about—private things—and it's embarrassing to have her hanging around.

What can I do to get her off my back?

Emily

> *I am giving you a new commandment:*
> *Love each other. Just as I have loved you,*
> *you should love each other.*
> John 13:34 NLT

My Brother, My Sister—My Friend?

The old principle is sad but true: the people we love the most are often the ones we hurt the most. Unfortunately, when I was a teenager, I applied this principle to my younger sister.

In reality, I loved her very much, but I was so wrapped up in my selfish desires that, most of the time, I treated her like some sort of "subhuman." I hate to admit it, but I took my frustrations out on her—I trampled over her when I was in a bad mood, and I yelled at her for no reason at all.

I'll never forget one night two weeks before I left for college. My dad pulled me aside and said something that has stuck with me to this day. He said, "Shelley, you are going away to school in a couple of weeks, and your sister thinks that you hate her." His words cut me like a knife; I felt truly horrible.

Of course I didn't hate my sister, but once I started thinking about it, I could see that I had sure acted like I did.

Family—Shelley

I started thinking back on my relationship with Robyn. She was eight years younger than I was, so about the time I turned thirteen, she was five or six and very impressionable. A little sister naturally wants to hang out with her older sister, but I wouldn't have it!

I remember one particular weekend when Robyn, my two cousins, and I were staying at my grandparents' house while our parents were out of town. My cousins were my age, and Robyn, of course, was much younger. My cousins and I got together and chose a particularly foul-mouthed name to call Robyn—and we called her this name all weekend long. Not only did we call her names, but we wouldn't let her be a part of anything we did. It finally got to be too much for a little girl to handle, and she went off by herself to a bedroom and cried.

My cousin Bruce was touched by her tears and apologized to her and tried to console her—but not me. Now I can hardly believe how hard-hearted I was. Suffice it to say, when our parents got home, we all got into big trouble for making Robyn's weekend miserable—especially me.

This was just one of many such episodes that Robyn still remembers and I still try to forget. How sad that these are the memories Robyn has of my teenage years. Such incidents were what caused my dad to speak so solemnly to me and invoke me to contemplate my actions. She and I are very close now, and although she has forgiven me, I still feel guilty over those years.

Sometimes I even find myself trying to make it up to her in some way. What I didn't realize then but what is so painfully clear to me now is that it is impossible to turn back time.

My Brother, My Sister—My Friend?

Why did I treat her so badly? I've tried to figure it out, and this is what I've come up with: Unlike people unrelated to me (like my friends), she couldn't disown me or walk away from me for good. After all, she was my sister—my own flesh and blood, so I felt I could treat her however I wanted. It just seemed like no big deal. She happened to be the closest, easiest "scapegoat." But you see, the very thing I thought justified my treating her so badly is the very thing that should have made me treat her the best of all, with the utmost love and respect. Because she is my flesh and blood, she is one of the few people who will actually remain with me throughout my whole life, one of the people I can trust the most. She—above all other friends—deserved my highest esteem. But that's not the way it went. I was just too immature to even give it a thought.

I'd venture to say that many of you are going through the very same thing—whether on the giving or receiving end. Every time we are out doing a concert and I see two siblings come through the line, I ask if they get along well. The answer is usually a strong "no!"

Why is it that we fight with our siblings like there's no tomorrow, but we're so utterly concerned about getting along with our friends? I remember walking on eggshells to avoid confrontation with my friends because I was so obsessed with their liking me, while going off on my sister without giving it a second thought.

Now, I'm sure some of you have wonderful relationships with your siblings—maybe you even consider them your best friends. You are very blessed—and very wise. But I'm also sure that many of you are like me, and with you I'd like to share two major things I'd do differently—if I had it to do over again.

1. Let your first thought be love. As a teenager, I used to listen to a Christian band called Whiteheart. One of their songs has always stuck with me. I don't remember the verses, but the chorus said, "Let your first thought, let your very first thought, be love…." Can you imagine how peacefully we could coexist with our brothers and sisters if we could train our hearts and mouths to employ this principle? When a brother or sister is nagging you or bothering you or doing something to make you mad, let your first thought be love. Now, I'll be the first to admit that this kind of response is not easy, but it is so much better than the alternative.

Ask yourself: What does love look like in this situation? A soft, sweet reply or turning the other cheek will work wonders. Or maybe you'll need to listen instead of slamming the door. Proverbs 15:1 reminds us that "a gentle answer turns away wrath, but a harsh word stirs up anger" (NIV).

When you and a brother or sister start in on each other, say a quick prayer: "Jesus, help my first thought be love, because I really do love this person." Just try it. Train yourself to take time to think and pray before you react. You won't always remember (I know, I've tried it on my husband!), but eventually God will bless your obedience, and a response of love might even become automatic and truly authentic.

2. Do something to serve your brothers and sisters at least once every day. This may seem impossible, but it doesn't have to be. It all goes back to the "Golden Rule" that you've heard all your life: "Do to others as you would have them do to you" (Matthew 7:12 NIV). I should have put it into practice with my sister.

My Brother, My Sister—My Friend?

For instance, I could have served my sister by sharing some of my "precious" time simply playing with her. I was a lot older than she and really didn't enjoy the games she liked, but fifteen minutes a day wouldn't have killed me, and it would have meant the world to her. Maybe you have an older brother. You could clean up his room or offer to clear off the table for him when it's his turn. It's little things like these that can add up to an awesome relationship.

But don't get discouraged if your siblings don't reciprocate. They have to be convinced just like you do.

Take a few minutes to contemplate your sibling relationships. Are they where they need to be? Or do they need a little work? When I was your age, no one but my parents ever suggested that I consider my relationship with my sister, and unfortunately, I didn't listen until I was leaving home. If sharing these thoughts with you can save you from the guilt and regret I felt the night my dad confronted me, I will have accomplished my purpose. Would your relationships be better if your first thought were love? Could you find ways to serve your brothers and sisters and actually treat them like friends?

Chances are, the answer is yes.

STUDY GUIDE

Who Is Watching You?

📖 **Opening Scripture:** Begin today's study by reading 1 Timothy 4:12. Ask God to speak to you in a specific way as you study His Word.

❀ **You Are a Role Model:** Have you ever thought about the fact that you are a role model? You may not have "signed up" for that assignment, but nonetheless, you are exactly that. Although you may not know it, there is someone who looks up to you. This person watches the way you talk and the way you behave on your best and worst days. If you have a younger sibling, you can be certain he or she looks up to you. Even if you have no younger siblings, there are others who are watching. They may be neighbors, family members, or friends.

What do you think? How does that make you feel?

❑ Who me? I don't believe that.

❑ Terrified. I hope no one is watching me.

❑ Proud. I would be the best role model someone could follow.

❑ Humble. I hope I do my best to guide others in the right way.

What's your experience? What would others learn from watching your life? _____

_____

_____

_____

Who Is Watching You?

✿ Don't Let Your Youth Hurt Your Example

Fill in the blanks: Reread 1 Timothy 4:12. Fill in the missing words:
"Don't let anyone look down on you because you are _____,
but set an example for the believers in _____, in _____,
in _____, in _____ and in _____."

What do you think? Why do you think it's easy for people to look down
on those younger than they are? _____

_____

_____

What can you do to prevent others from looking down on you
because you are younger than they are? _____

_____

_____

Think about it: This verse calls us to set an example in several areas of
our lives. We are to live in such a way that we are worthy of
imitation. Is your life one that should be imitated by those younger
than you? Why or why not? _____

_____

_____

_____

✿ How You Can Set an Example: First Timothy 4:12 calls us to set
an example in five areas.

Family—Study Guide

1. Speech. The words that come out of our mouths have such power—to do good or harm. Consider the example you are to others in what you say.

Fill in the blanks: Read Proverbs 31:26 and fill in the missing words: "She speaks with _____, and faithful instruction is on her _____."

What's your experience? How much of the time does this statement describe you?

- ❏ Most of the time
- ❏ Are you kidding? Hardly ever.
- ❏ I try my best to grow each day.
- ❏ Every second of every day

What do you think? What are some ways you could change your words in order to be a better example?_____

_____

_____

Think about it: Are you setting an example in what you say within your family? It is easy to be careless in our words at home. We often take our families for granted and treat them worse than we do strangers. The real test of a Christian is how she speaks to her family at home.

2. Life. God has called Christians to live holy lives. It is a high calling, but it is possible when we rely on His power.

Who Is Watching You?

What does the Word say? Read Ephesians 4:1. Are there choices you need to make in order to live as He commands? If so, what are they?

_____

_____

_____

_____

3. Love. Maybe you have heard the old saying "People don't care how much you know until they know how much you care." Our love for people should set us apart as disciples of Jesus. Without it, everything else we do is just a waste of time.

What does the Word say? Read Ephesians 4:2. Why is love important in setting an example?_____

_____

_____

According to this verse, what are some actions that demonstrate our love for others? _____

_____

Think about it: Do you treat those closest to you lovingly? What about those who have harmed you? Do you model a servant heart or a "me-first" attitude? The more you grow in your relationship with Christ, the more loving you will become as God changes you from the inside out.

4. Faith. Many people claim their faith is private and not to be discussed with others. While our faith is personal, it should never stay private. Our faith should penetrate every area of life. As others watch you, do they see the difference your faith in Jesus makes? They should.

What does the Word say? Read Hebrews 11:6. What does this passage say God will do for those who earnestly seek Him?

- ❑ He gives them joy.
- ❑ He rewards them.
- ❑ He hides from them.
- ❑ He teaches them.

What do you think? What do you think it means for someone to earnestly seek Him? _____

_____

_____

How do you think God rewards those who seek Him? _____

_____

_____

Think about it: When others watch your life, can they see that you are seeking after God?

5. Purity. It doesn't take long to figure out that purity is under attack these days. It is laughed at on TV and in the movies and is considered outdated and impossible. But it is possible through God's strength.

Who Is Watching You?

What does the Word say? Read 1 Corinthians 6:18–20. According to these verses, what is your body?

❏ A work in progress

❏ Hard to control

❏ A temple of the Holy Spirit

❏ Trying to get me in constant trouble

Knowing this, how should you treat your body? _____

_____

_____

_____

Think about it: Will you commit to grow in purity? Purity is simply living according to the truth of God's Word. If so, you must guard your thoughts, your emotions, and your body.

What practical steps will you take to remain committed to purity?

_____

_____

_____

_____

_____

_____

✔ **Try This:** List one person you know who looks up to you.

_____

Family—Study Guide

Write one practical step you will take this week to be a godly role model in this person's life. _____

_____

_____

_____

_____

Remember, others will follow the footprints you leave behind. Make it your goal to lead them closer to Christ.

✝ **Living the Word:** Read Luke 17:1–2.

• What does Jesus say about those who cause others to sin? _____

_____

_____

• To whom do you think the passage is referring when it speaks of "little ones"? _____

_____

_____

_____

• What are some ways we cause others to sin? _____

_____

_____

_____

_____

Who Is Watching You?

• How are you careful to avoid setting a bad example? _____

_____

_____

• Your influence can be used for good or bad. Will you choose to leave a legacy of holiness? _____

Dear Point of Grace,

I think my parents are getting a divorce. They fight almost every night, and they say the most horrible things to each other. I hate it when they yell. I just stay in my room and pray that they will be nice to each other.

The other night they were fighting because I wanted some money for new jeans to wear to a party. First they fought about how much money I was allowed to spend on clothes, and then they fought about whether or not I should be allowed to go to the party. Hearing them fight makes me feel like it's all my fault.

I can't stand the thought of not having one of them in my home. It feels like it's me that's splitting up, not them. Why doesn't God answer my prayers to keep them together, or does He even care about things like this?

Julie

A father to the fatherless,
a defender of widows,
is God in his holy dwelling.
Psalm 68:5 NIV

A Father to the Fatherless

I know I'm stating the obvious, but not all families are happy. Not every family is made up of Mom, Dad, two kids, and a dog. Not every home is a safe, secure place to be. Some of you are dealing with the pain of divorce or abandonment by a parent. Some of you live with non-Christian parents or simply feel unloved. Others of you may be in situations of serious abuse (emotional or physical) and really need help beyond this book. (I'll talk a little about that later.) If you're struggling with any of these situations or feelings, this devotional is for you.

Because I came from such a good home, at first I felt intimidated about even approaching this subject. But as I thought about it, I realized that God and His Word supply us with some basic truths that are helpful no matter who the "messenger" (me) is.

1. God cares. The first truth I want to share is that God cares! First Peter 5:7 says it so beautifully: "Cast all your anxiety on him because he cares for you" (NIV). God knows all about you and your heartaches. He even knows how many hairs are on your head. Luke 12:6–7 explains our value to God this way: "Are not five sparrows sold for two pennies? Yet not one of them is forgotten by God. Indeed, the very hairs of your head are all numbered. Don't be afraid; you are worth more than many sparrows" (NIV). God cares for you.

2. Jesus understands. Imagine if you had a friend who *always* understood what you were going through. I mean, *really* understood—even had been through it herself. And when you talked to her, she was all ears, comforting you, never saying, "Let me call you back" or "I can't help you with this one. It's too messy." Imagine a person who was so consistent in her friendship that she seemed perfect. Sound impossible? It is! No earthly friend could be that good, but Jesus can. Jesus is a friend who really understands.

In fact, Hebrews 4:15 says this about Jesus, our High Priest: "This High Priest of ours understands our weaknesses, for he faced all of the same temptations we do, yet he did not sin" (NLT). Do you get that? He sympathizes with us, and He understands how we feel. He understands how it feels to be betrayed, lonely, and mistreated. He understands because He has been there.

3. God works all things together for good. Even though God cares very much for us, bad things still happen. I don't know all the answers to why God allows our parents to divorce, our dads to walk out, abuse to take place, or innocent children to suffer for things that are totally out of their control. I do know that Satan has *some* power in this world, and I know that all the evil in this world originates with him.

But God has *ultimate* power. Though Satan brings pain and suffering into this world, God will ultimately bring good. One of my very favorite promises in the Bible is in Romans 8:28: "We know that all things work together for good to those who love God, and to those who are the called according to His purpose" (NKJV). This verse doesn't say that only good things will happen to you. It says that God will work everything *together* for good.

There will be times in your life when you experience pain you never thought possible. There will be times when bad things happen to you. At those times, you must reach out and claim the promise of Romans 8:28. You must believe that God is weaving all the circumstances of your life into a gorgeous tapestry. On the backside, you can see mistakes and backstitches and ugly knots, but on the front, you see a beautiful arrangement of color and design.

4. Fervent prayer is effective. Our friend Jesus will help us through any and every thing that life sends our way, but we need to *ask* for that help through prayer. When our world throws us problems that we didn't sign up for, we need to throw ourselves on Him.

Jesus wants us to talk to Him about our problems, and this applies to problems at home. But we must come to Him in fervent prayer. *Fervent* means "extremely passionate enthusiasm." James 5:16 says that "the effective, fervent prayer of a righteous man avails much" (NKJV).

Fervent prayer is *not* just throwing up a quick, mindless prayer and expecting our problems to vanish. Fervent prayer means taking the time to really pour our hearts out to God with an attitude of submission to Him and a willingness to learn what *we* can do to make a difference. Fervent prayer takes real energy and can even be hard work.

I've discovered that it's only when I pray fervently and wholeheartedly—with everything in me—that I sense His true presence and comfort and an overall feeling that everything is going to be okay.

5. God is a father to the fatherless. Psalm 68:5–6 says that God is a "father to the fatherless" and a "defender of widows." What a beautiful picture of a loving God. It goes on to say that He "places the lonely in families" and "sets the prisoners free and gives them joy" (NLT). Isn't that what we want when we feel lonely—to be part of a family, to belong? And have you ever felt like a prisoner in your home circumstances? This verse says that God sets prisoners free and gives them joy.

There are other places in the Bible that talk about God's special love and care for the fatherless: Deuteronomy 10:18 says, "He defends the cause of the fatherless and the widow" (NIV), and 24:17 says, "Do not deprive the alien or the fatherless of justice" (NIV). Proverbs 23:10–11 warns, "Do not move an ancient boundary stone or encroach on the fields of the fatherless, for their Defender is strong; he will take up their case against you" (NIV). Psalm 27:10 says, "Even if my father and mother abandon me, the LORD will hold me close" (NLT).

Do you get the feeling that God has a special place in His heart for those who are without a father or mother? Can't you hear His compassion and protection ringing loudly from those scriptures?

A Father to the Fatherless

It's just my opinion, but I've always thought that God has something extraspecial in mind for those who don't have an earthly father, that He will show Himself to them in an awesome way reserved only for them.

6. Obey even non-Christian parents. I often hear the question "Do I still have to obey my parents if they're not Christians?" The answer is *yes*—absolutely. God calls us to be loving, obedient children whether or not our parents are believers. The ultimate goal is that through prayer and our example that they, too, will come to Christ. This is unlikely if your example as a Christian includes disobedience.

Now, there is an exception to this. In extreme circumstances, children are sometimes asked to do things that are wrong or that use their bodies in a way not intended by God. If this is happening to you, you must tell someone immediately and get some help. Go to an adult friend you trust—a pastor, a teacher, or a parent of a friend. But tell someone. Mercy Ministries of America (1-800-922-9131) is a group that can direct you to someone in your area who can help you, and your call to them will be completely confidential.

7. Your parents' problems are not your fault. It's important that you understand that you have absolutely no control over what happens between your mom and dad. You don't have the power to make them stay married or the power to pull them apart. You only have control over how *you* deal with the broken pieces. As unfair as that sounds, that's how life is. We don't get to pick and choose what comes our way, but we do get to choose how we respond.

Family—Shelley

God designed families as a place for people to grow and learn about love, sharing, sacrifice, and much more. He also designed families to provide love and security to all their members. And when families don't work as God intended, pain results. God knows this and is ready to comfort us.

Maybe your parents are divorced, and you don't have a mom or dad who is there for you. Maybe you've never even known your father or mother. Or maybe your parents are both in your home, but they aren't Christians, and this makes you feel alone.

Whatever your circumstances, God is on your side. He is for you. He is closer than you think. Satan would love nothing more than to use the problems in your family to thwart your relationship with God. *Don't let him do it!*

With God's help, you can turn your circumstances around for good and become more like Jesus in the process. How can living through your parents' divorce make you more like Jesus? I believe that pain can make you stronger in character, more sympathetic to others with similar problems, and, most important, more dependent on God—who is the best and most perfect parent we could ever want.

STUDY GUIDE

Making the Best of Your Situation

📖 **Opening Scripture:** Pray that God speaks to you in a specific way today as you study His Word. Read Philippians 4:12.

❧ **The Secret of Contentment:** Not every home is an ideal one, and many things in your home are not under your control. You can't fix other people. But you can learn to be content in whatever situation you find yourself.

Fill in the blanks: Reread Philippians 4:12 and fill in the missing words: "I know what it is to be in _____, and I know what it is to have _____. I have learned the _____ of being _____ in any and every _____."

What's your experience? What about your family life is not ideal?_____
_____
_____

Have you learned any "secrets" about being content in your situation? Write them here: _____
_____
_____

Pray about it: Commit to praying for each member of your family. As you do this, you will begin to see them through Jesus' eyes. Prayer changes our focus from the present to eternity and helps us be more content.

If any of your family members don't know Christ, ask God to draw them to Himself. Pray that they will become aware of their need for salvation.

Think about it: Prayer breeds thankfulness in our hearts, and thankfulness breeds contentment. Read Philippians 1:3–4. How can praying for those in your family help you be more content with them?

❧ **Acknowledge Every Day as a Gift from God:** A person who makes the best of her situation uses the opportunities God places in front of her. She acknowledges that each day is a gift from God. She unwraps it carefully and honors Him in the way she treats this gift.

Fill in the blanks: Psalm 118:24: "This is the ____ the Lord has made; let us _____ and be _____ in it."

Think about it: What things about your family can you rejoice and be glad about? _____

_____

❧ **Living for a Higher Purpose:** As we learn to make the best of our situations, we must sometimes relinquish the right to live for our own will and satisfaction and live for a higher purpose—serving others.

Family—Study Guide

Fill in the blanks: Read Matthew 10:39. Fill in the missing words: "Whoever _____ his life will lose it, and whoever loses his life for my sake _____."

Think about it: This verse is not talking about literal life and death. Instead, it refers to the goals and motives we have for our lives. When we live for our own satisfaction and happiness, we will only become emptier. On the other hand, when we seek to please our Master first, we will find purpose and freedom.

What's your experience? Have you ever sacrificed your own happiness to serve another and found joy in the process? If so, describe that experience. _____

_____

✿ **Learning to Get Along:** Read Philippians 2:1–4. What do you think verse 2 means when it calls us to be "like-minded"?
   ❏ Totally alike in every belief and idea
   ❏ Striving toward unity with others in the body of Christ
   ❏ Open-minded
   ❏ Focused on the truth of God's Word

What do you think? What are some practical ways you can become more like-minded with others in your family even though you may not agree with them 100 percent of the time? _____

_____

_____

_____

✿ Putting Others First

Fill in the blanks: Reread Philippians 2:3. Fill in the missing words: "Do _____ out of selfish ambition or vain conceit, but in _____ consider others _____ than yourselves."

Think about it: Ouch! This verse may seem impossible, but when we rely on God's power, we find the strength necessary to obey. Followers of Jesus put others first. They seek to live this way every day. Of course they aren't perfect, but when they mess up, they ask for forgiveness and move on.

What do you think? What is the most challenging thing about putting others first? _____

_____

_____

_____

What's your experience? Do you know someone who consistently puts others first? If so, describe the impact that person has on those around them. _____

_____

_____

_____

Think about it: You will not have your family forever. Someday you will no longer share a home with them. Will you commit to serve your family while you have the chance? If so, begin today.

How often do you serve the people in your family?

❏ I do this all the time.

❏ I do this often, but I could do it even more.

❏ I can't remember the last time I did this.

❏ I rarely do this, but I want to change.

Philippians 2:4 says to look to others' interests. Make a list of the people in your family. Next to each name write down this person's interests and concerns. List some practical actions you can take to support this person. _____

_____

_____

_____

✔ **Try This:** Find a picture of your entire family. It might be a picture from last Christmas or one from a recent vacation.

Take a few moments to really look at the faces in that picture. What do you see? Do you see those with whom you constantly fight? Do you see those who have hurt you?

Take some time to prayerfully look at that picture and ask God to give you His perspective about the members of your family. Did you know that He loves each one dearly? He sent His Son to die for every person in that picture. Will you choose to allow God's perspective to influence the way you treat the people in that picture?

Place this picture somewhere so you will see it each day. You may even want to put it in your Bible. Will you commit to pray daily for the people in this picture? If so, sign your name in the space provided.

_____

✞ **Living the Word:** Read Philippians 2:5–8.
• Describe the attitude of Jesus Christ as shown in these verses.

_____

_____

_____

• In what ways can you choose to have the same attitude in your daily life? _____

_____

_____

• Is there something specific you can do today to adopt the role of a servant in your family? If so, what is it? _____

_____

_____

_____

_____

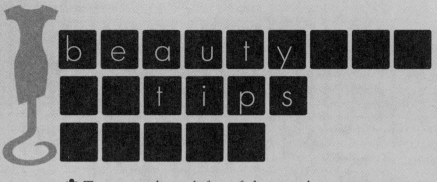

beauty tips

❀ To prevent lipstick from fading, apply foundation to lips, then blot. Apply lip liner and blot. Apply lipstick and blot again.

❀ When applying blush, less is more. Look in the mirror and smile widely to find the apple of the cheek. With short, light strokes apply blush to the apple.

❀ To shape nails, choose the shape that is best for your nails. If you have an oval-shaped cuticle at the base, the square look works well. If your cuticles are pointed, an oval-shaped nail looks best.

❀ Curling your eyelashes helps open up the face. Even if you don't use much makeup, this can be a very useful tool.

❀ Leave the last cookie/piece of bread/scoop of ice cream for someone else. Offer it to your brother, sister, parent, or friend.

❀ Respect your family's privacy by keeping their embarrassing habits to yourself—no matter how funny they are.

❀ Respond with a soft answer when you are in a discussion that makes you angry—no matter how wrong others' opinions are.

❀ If your family doesn't pray each morning before school, ask them to join you in a before-school prayer time—don't be afraid to be a leader. The worst that could happen is that they will say no, and you'll be no worse off than before.

inner beauty tips

friends

Dear Point of Grace,

I feel like no one cares about me. I mean, I'm pretty sure it's not true, but it's still the way I feel. It even seems that my best friend doesn't care about me! I'm not the type of person who shares my feelings with others. This has been a problem for me. I'm afraid to let anyone get close to me. I'm afraid of getting hurt.

I know God is always right beside me and that He is my closest friend, but I still feel lonely and sad. I want to make new friends, but I don't even know what kind of friend to look for. Can you help me?

April

A friend loves at all times,
and a brother is born for adversity.
Proverbs 17:17 NIV

What a Friend Is

What is a friend? There are probably as many definitions of *friend* as there are girls reading this book. *The Student Bible* says that friends know, like, and trust one another; they support and sympathize with each other. Isn't that what we all want in a friend? Someone who knows us and likes us anyway. Someone we can trust with our most secret secrets; someone who'll support us when we feel like we're falling apart; someone who'll feel our pain with us.

When I look back on my life, some of my very best memories are times spent with friends. Just thinking about them makes me smile and brings warmth to my heart. Friends have given me laughter in my tears, joy in my sorrow, and unconditional love when I felt completely unlovable. It's not how *many* friends we have that matters, but the precious *qualities* of those friends. Listen to what the Bible says in Proverbs 18:24 (I've paraphrased it just a little): "A girl of many friends may come to ruin, but a really good friend sticks closer than a sister." What this means is that you need a couple of close friends with whom you can share your real self, rather than many friends who won't stick with you through thick and thin.

When I think about the friends who've meant the most to me throughout my life, I see several characteristics that make them my "true" friends. Let's look at what it takes to make a real friend. A good friend is:

1. Loyal and Trustworthy. Hear me when I say this: a good friend does not talk harmfully about a friend behind her back. I have felt the pain of this in my own life. It may seem innocent and even fun, but it will kill a friendship fast. Real friends do not tell each others' secrets. A real friend is someone to whom you can tell *anything*—even something that would make great "gossip"—without fear that she will betray your trust.

You may think it's impossible to be a truly faithful friend at this stage in your life, but it's not. "A gossip goes around revealing secrets, but those who are trustworthy can keep a confidence" (Proverbs 11:13 NLT).

2. Honest. Being honest with our friends isn't always easy, but it is so important. If we let hurt feelings and misunderstandings go unresolved, they will fester in our hearts, and bitterness and distrust will take root. I am very honest with my friends—sometimes maybe even a little too blunt. But it is this honesty that has allowed us to remain friends. I tell my friends when they hurt me, and they tell me when I hurt them. I can count on them to call me out on a wrong. We hold each other accountable. Proverbs 27:5–6 says, "An open rebuke is better than hidden love! Wounds from a friend are better than many kisses from an enemy" (NLT).

What a Friend Is

In learning how to be honest but kind, a good place to start is Ephesians 4:15. It tells us to *speak the truth in love*. This simple rule will help you know when and how to tell a possibly painful truth. Honesty doesn't mean spouting off out of anger or just to get things "off our chest." Truth must always be tempered by love.

3. Forgiving. Unconditional forgiveness is key to any relationship. In marriage you have to forgive even when you think you're right or have been hurt. Consider friendship a practice for your future marriage. Ephesians 4:32 says, "Be kind to each other, tenderhearted, forgiving one another, just as God through Christ has forgiven you" (NLT). We all mess up—often! None of us likes to admit our imperfections, but being aware of our weaknesses helps us to be forgiving of the imperfections in others. If we expect our friendships to last, we must forgive and ask for forgiveness. Even the most hurtful things can be forgiven and put to rest.

4. Spiritually Encouraging and Supportive. Kind words from my closest friends help my self-esteem and encourage me spiritually more than almost anything else. You can encourage your friends by little things you say and do. Tell your friends how sweet, caring, and precious they are. Tell them how cute they look or that you love a new outfit. Focus on your friends' inner qualities, too—like their kindness or great attitude in a difficult time.

Seek out friends who share your Christian beliefs. If we don't hang out with spiritually uplifting friends, we will drown in our walk with God. You cannot be a godly girl all alone. Hebrews 3:13 talks about encouraging each other: "Encourage one another daily, as long as it is still called Today, so that none of you may be hardened by sin's deceitfulness" (NIV). When Jesus is the foundation of a friendship, it will go much deeper than any other friendship.

There's a special kind of encouragement called "accountability." This means that you "answer" to a friend for how you behave on a date or how you're doing in your relationship with God. When you're accountable to someone, you are obligated, in a sense, to share openly with her about how things *really* are with you—and she shares how things are with her. I encourage you to choose someone in your life—someone who is trustworthy—to be your accountability partner. If you'll do this, you'll be challenged to grow in ways you may never be able to grow alone.

5. A Good Listener. If all we do is talk, not many people will want to be around us. A true friend is skilled in the art of listening. When our friends share problems with us, our first instinct is to try to "fix" things. But sometimes the very best thing we can do is be quiet and just listen. I struggle with this one because advice just seems to flow out of my mouth. Most of the time, what is really needed is my attentive heart and my prayers. "Do you see a [girl] who speaks in haste? There is more hope for a fool than for [her]" (Proverbs 29:20 NIV). James 1:19 says, "Be quick to listen, slow to speak" (NIV). My best advice on this topic is that you should pray and not talk. If a friend asks for your advice, be wise in giving your opinion. If the problem is a serious one, you might need to direct your friend to your youth minister or pastor.

6. Someone You Can Be Yourself with—All the Time. There is no greater joy than feeling free enough to completely let your guard down with a friend. My husband, Chris, and a small group of girlfriends are the only people I really do that with. I am not saying I'm not myself around other people, but when I'm with these people, I know they will love me no matter how I am. When I know I am not being judged, I know I am with a friend. I've heard it said that "True friends are the ones who really know you but love you anyway." I like that.

7. Available. Imagine having a "friend" who announced that she was available only on Fridays and Tuesday mornings. You would think she was crazy. It's not fun to ask someone to do things with you and always get turned down. I have friends whom I can call at any hour of the day or night and know that they will be instantly available to me. Of course, we can't abuse this aspect of friendship and demand all of our friends' time, but real friends are available to each other and care about each others' needs. "Each of you should look not only to your own interests, but also to the interests of others" (Philippians 2:4 NIV). Being interested in and available to your friends will shape you into a "best" friend.

8. Giving and Helpful. "God loves a cheerful giver" (2 Corinthians 9:7 NIV). When a friend is in trouble, don't annoy her by asking what you can do; figure out something helpful and do it. When you were a baby, you were naturally selfish. You were helpless and demanded that others do everything for you. But now you are at a time in your life when you need to be unselfish. It's time to look at a friend and see what she needs rather than focusing on what you need from her. Learn the art of giving unselfishly, and you will truly be happy.

9. Godly. When you hang out with the wrong people, you will have more problems than the friendships are worth. Trust me on this: Don't get caught up with people who are bad influences. "Do not be misled: 'Bad company corrupts good character'" (1 Corinthians 15:33 NIV). Friendship with such people will only be temporary, and the wrong kinds of friends can bring you great heartbreak. You know when someone is a bad influence. Use your head to be strong and wise. "Be careful how you live, not as fools but as those who are wise" (Ephesians 5:15 NLT). "Fear the LORD and shun evil" (Proverbs 3:7 NIV). Search out friends who share your belief in God. We don't want to shun people, but we must be wise in who we allow to influence us.

10. Someone Who Laughs with You. Laughter is medicine to your soul. The wise King Solomon tells us in Ecclesiates 3:1 and 4 that "There is a time for everything, and a season for every activity under heaven…a time to weep and a time to laugh, a time to mourn and a time to dance" (NIV). Friends are people we share good times with. We connect with them through tears and through laughter. Ethel Barrymore said that "you grow up the day you have the first real laugh at yourself." How true. People who are sure enough of themselves to laugh at their shortcomings are relaxing to be with. Laughter reminds us not to take life too seriously. I love the feeling of laughing when I feel like falling apart. It releases stress to have a good laugh with friends.

Now that you know what a true friend is made of, you know what to look for in others, and you know what to strive for in your own life.

STUDY GUIDE

Friends to Encourage Me

📖 **Opening Scripture:** Ask God to speak to you in a specific way as you study His Word. Then read Proverbs 13:20.

❂ **"Identical" Friends:** Has anyone ever seen you with your best friend and pointed out how alike the two of you are? Maybe they noticed that you wear your hair the same way, talk alike, or have the same sense of humor. Good friends often tend to share the same tastes, interests, and dreams. Why is this so? Friends "rub off" on each other. They influence each other in ways that are obvious and in others that aren't quite as easy to see.

What's your experience? List one way that you and a good friend are alike. _____

❂ **The Power of a Friend's Influence:** Friends can influence us for the better, as well as for the worse. Sometimes they bring out the best in us and challenge us to grow.

What's your experience? Describe one instance when a friend influenced you for the better. _____

At other times friends can cause us to compromise our standards and lose sight of what is best for our lives. Describe a time when a friend's influence caused you to behave in a way you later regretted.

106

_____

_____

✿ Walk with the Wise

What does the Word say? Reread Proverbs 13:20. What do you think this verse means by "walking with the wise"?

- ❏ Running a marathon next to someone extremely intelligent
- ❏ Carefully selecting friends who live according to biblical standards
- ❏ Never associating with people who are non-Christians
- ❏ Always keeping our eyes and ears open to see what is around us

When the Bible speaks of "walking with" someone, it refers to allowing that person close access into our lives. It means the more time we spend with people, the more they will influence us.

What's your experience? Which of your friends has the greatest influence on you? _____

Think about it: Do you walk with the wise? Do your friends encourage you to follow Christ and become more like Him? If so, you will find that the more time you spend with them, the more you will grow in your relationship with Christ. On the other hand, if your friends constantly laugh at your faith or tempt you to compromise, the more time you spend with them, the more you will drift in your commitment to Christ.

Friends—Study Guide

✿ Unwise Relationships

Fill in the blanks: Fill in the missing words from Proverbs 13:20: "A
_____ of fools suffers_____."

What do you think? In what ways could you suffer harm by being
friends with those who are foolish? _____

_____

_____

_____

Pray about it: In reading this, you may have realized you have some
friends who are causing you harm. If so, you probably need to limit
the time you spend with them. Ask God to help you replace
unhealthy friendships with friends who encourage you in your walk
with Him. This doesn't mean you never speak to your old friends
again; it just means you reduce the influence they have over you.

You may want to make different choices about the activities you
participate in with them. Start praying for God to soften their hearts
to His love. Take opportunities He gives you to share with them.
You can still be involved in their lives, but your closest friends
should be those who encourage you to walk with Him.

✿ Friendly Encouragement: Read Hebrews 3:12–13. The word
encouragement literally means "to breathe courage into another."
What's your experience? List some people you know who encourage you
in your walk with Christ. _____

Friends to Encourage Me

_____

_____

What do you think? In what ways can you follow the command in this verse to "encourage one another daily"? _____

_____

What warning do you find in the passage? _____

_____

What's your experience? How can encouragement keep us from becoming "hardened by sin's deceitfulness"? _____

_____

_____

_____

_____

✿ **Enjoy Being Part of a Church Family:** God never intended for us to walk the journey of faith alone. He provides Christian friends, mentors, and leaders to help us as we seek to become more like Christ. His will is for you to be involved in a local church where you learn about His Word and live in unity with other Christians.

What does the Word say? Read Hebrews 10:24–25. Why is it so important that Christians don't give up meeting with one another?

_____

_____

❀ **Meet with an Accountability Group:** In addition to participating in a church that teaches God's Word, you may also consider meeting together with a group of friends for the purpose of spiritual growth. Girls will use any excuse to get together, right? Well, why not ask some friends to form an accountability group with you?

An ideal group consists of anywhere from three to six girls who also want to grow in their relationships with Christ. You might decide to meet once a week to discuss what God is teaching each of you. You can also share struggles and areas where you need to grow. Accountability partners pray with and for each other. They keep a high level of trust, knowing that the things shared in confidence will be treated with discretion.

What's your experience? Read James 5:16. How vulnerable can you be with your Christian friends about your personal struggles?

❏ I feel like I must constantly put on an act that I am doing okay.

❏ My friends don't have the time to listen to my silly problems.

❏ If I opened up to my friends, they would pray for me and support me.

❏ I don't have a Christian friend whom I could go to about a problem.

Pray about it: Christian friends make all the difference during the hard times in life. They point us to Christ and support us by praying for us. If you do not have friends like this, start praying for some today.

Friends to Encourage Me

✔ **Try This:** Write down the names of three people you know who may be interested in forming an accountability group. Ask them this week to pray about whether they would like to be involved. If you do not know anyone right now whom you think would be interested, pray and wait. God will faithfully bring the right people in the right time. _____

✝ **Living the Word:** Read Proverbs 27:17.

• Just as iron is sharpened by constant friction rubbing against it, we are challenged as we allow our lives to be closely connected with other Christians. How has God used someone else to make you "sharper"?

• We must be vulnerable in order to have our lives challenged by others. How easy is it for you to be honest about your needs and shortcomings? _____

• What practical steps can you take that will assure you will be sharpened by other Christians? _____

_____

_____

Dear Point of Grace,

How am I supposed to find a real friend when most of the girls I've been friends with have stabbed me in the back? Sometimes girls can be so evil to each other. How can I find a true friend?

It seems like the people I get along with best are the people who end up getting me into trouble. How do I know what kind of friends to choose?

Erin

Don't think only about your own affairs, but be interested in others, too, and what they are doing.
Philippians 2:4 NLT

What a Friend Isn't

In my last devotional, we talked about what a true friend is. Now we need to talk about what a friend isn't. The way I see it, the five biggest problem areas in teenage friendships are gossip, criticism, cliques, jealousy, and trying to please others so much that you sacrifice what is right. Let's see what the Bible says about these areas and shed some light on areas you may need to work on.

Gossip. Okay. Let's be honest. We all gossip to some extent. Some of it may seem harmless, but I'll bet you've had some experiences where it was very harmful—whether you were the one being gossiped about or the one doing the gossiping. And while we're being honest, let's just go ahead and admit that we sometimes gossip about others to gain popularity or to make ourselves look good. And the truth is, sharing a juicy piece of gossip sometimes gets you on the "inside," but only for a moment.

There are two kinds of gossip: telling a lie about someone and telling something that was told to you in confidence. Both of these will ruin a friendship faster than anything else. Proverbs 16:28 says that "gossip separates the best of friends" (NLT). Now, think about it: if your friend gossips about other people, why wouldn't she gossip about you? If she constantly talks bad about others when they aren't around, what makes you think she doesn't talk about you when you're not around? If you can't trust a friend, why continue the relationship? Let's turn this around for a minute: if others can't trust *you*, why should they want to be *your* friend?

The damage that gossip does is hard to repair. "It's harder to make amends with an offended friend than to capture a fortified city. Arguments separate friends like a gate locked with iron bars" (Proverbs 18:19 NLT). That is a pretty heavy verse. A fortified city and iron bars cannot be easily broken into—that is how hard it would be to restore a friendship after gossip has separated it.

The power of our words is almost frightening. "The tongue is a small thing, but what enormous damage it can do. A tiny spark can set a great forest on fire. And the tongue is a flame of fire. It is full of wickedness that can ruin your whole life" (James 3:5–6 NLT). If we can learn to keep our fiery tongues under control, we can gain a reputation as a trustworthy person. Proverbs 11:13 says, "Those who are trustworthy can keep a confidence" (NLT). But if we don't control our tongues, the Bible also tells us in Proverbs 25:10 that we will have a hard time regaining our reputation once we are pegged as a gossip.

Don't gossip; don't even listen to gossip. Defend your friends, and they will defend you.

Criticism. Okay, we're probably all feeling a bit guilty right now, so let's move on to criticism. This, like gossip, can seem harmless, but it cuts like a knife. Sometimes what we mean as an "innocent" joke can really hurt. Maybe we're just goofing around when we tell a friend, "You're so stupid," but our words can throw daggers into the hearts of others. Most people are hurt by that kind of joking, but some don't show it. They don't want to give you another reason to criticize them. Do you joke too much?

All of us are insecure at times. So work at being sensitive to the feelings of others, even if it is not natural for you. Use self-control in your choice of words. Stop and think before you blurt out your thoughts. Think about how you would feel if someone said to you what you say to them. Negative criticism may sometimes seem fun, but others will learn not to trust you if you are constantly critical. Be encouraging, and you will be trusted and well liked.

Let this prayer from God's Word be in your heart always: "May the words of my mouth and the thoughts of my heart be pleasing to you, O LORD, my rock and my redeemer" (Psalm 19:14 NLT).

Cliques. Webster's dictionary defines a *clique* as "a narrow, exclusive circle or group of persons; especially one held together by common interests, views, or purposes." Now, according to that definition, cliques aren't all bad. We can find security and acceptance in a group of people who share our interests and purposes. I still remember my high school days and how glad I was to belong to a group as I went to awkward dances and football games. But what makes a clique bad is when it is exclusive—and this happens a lot at school and, yes, even at church. Cliques are often made up of the "popular" kids, and they exclude people who aren't pretty enough or popular enough.

Friends—Terry

I remember seeing the cliques at my high school and wanting to be popular, too. I think it is natural to want to be liked. Thankfully, though, I didn't hang out with the most popular "in crowd." I saved myself a lot of heartache by not striving to be popular and by just being myself. I hung out with the choir and a few handpicked buddies who loved me for me and not because of how I looked or how talented I was. I also did a lot with our youth group, and it was a wonderful blend of all different kinds of neat Christian kids. They accepted me, and I accepted them. What was great about that group was that what held us together was Jesus.

Being a follower of Jesus often means doing things the hard way. It means befriending those who are left out of all the other groups—it means being kind to the unlovable. These people don't have to be your closest friends, but Jesus tells us that loving those who love us is really no big deal. He asks us to love those who don't love us: "If you love those who love you, what credit is that to you? For even 'sinners' love those who love them. And if you do good to those who do good to you, what credit is that to you? For even 'sinners' do that" (Luke 6:32–33 NIV). We are called to love people who are hard to love, not just the popular kids.

I was the kid nobody knew when I was a ninth-grader in a new school in Oklahoma. But there was a girl there who reached out to me and became one of my best friends. She later became my maid of honor, and she and I are still close friends today. Marti and I had some classes together, and she noticed that I was alone. She started by asking me to eat lunch with her. She got me involved in choir simply by inviting me and assuring me that I would like it. Simple efforts, but they made the world of difference to me.

Her kindness inspired me to do the same for others at school and church. I hope some of them remember me with the same fondness and appreciation that I have for Marti. You, too, can be remembered as the person who befriended someone who was alone—even though he or she wasn't popular or pretty or whatever.

Look at your own situation. Do you have a group you hang out with? Did you choose your group because they can make you look good? Do you exclude those who aren't quite cool enough? The words of the apostle Paul in the Book of Philippians give us some serious guidelines to consider when it comes to the people we hang out with: "Don't be selfish; don't live to make a good impression on others. Be humble, thinking of others as better than yourself. Don't think only about your own affairs, but be interested in others, too, and what they are doing" (2:3–4 NLT).

True friends don't look for what they can get out of other people or how good other people make them look. True friends see others through the eyes of God.

Jealousy. Another thing I see us girls struggle with is jealousy. We want what someone else has. It is so easy for us to see the good things about someone else and not recognize our own qualities.

We are jealous of superficial things like clothes, hair, body types, and money; but we are also jealous of people who have a lot of friends or a great personality. Jealousy is a poison that can eat away at the good inside of you until it eventually overcomes your thoughts. Proverbs 14:30 says, "A heart at peace gives life to the body, but envy rots the bones" (NIV).

You can't control everything in your life, but you can control whether or not you allow jealousy into your heart. One of the best ways to get jealousy out of your heart is to replace it with memorized scriptures like James 3:16–17: "Wherever there is jealousy and selfish ambition, there you will find disorder and every kind of evil. But the wisdom that comes from heaven is first of all pure. It is also peace loving, gentle at all times, and willing to yield to others. It is full of mercy and good deeds. It shows no partiality and is always sincere" (NLT).

Another great way to keep jealousy out of your heart is to be concerned for and help others. Jealousy and selfishness often go hand in hand. I ask you to look outside your own life for a bit. Ask what you can do for others, take the focus off yourself, and your jealousy will dwindle. Fill your mind with helping others and think on good things. Philippians 4:8 tells us, "Whatever is true, whatever is noble, whatever is right, whatever is pure, whatever is lovely, whatever is admirable—if anything is excellent or praiseworthy—think about such things" (NIV).

Be content with what you have, set goals that build on what God has given you, and focus on giving more than getting. Try to be happy for people when they do or receive something good, and you will be happier yourself.

Trying to Please Others. Finally, a friend is not someone who puts pressure on you to do something you know is wrong. Some people call this peer pressure; I call it trying too hard to please others. The Bible is our best source for knowing what is right and wrong. Beyond that, most of us have a basic instinct—a conscience—that tells us what's right and what's wrong. Use your head, and don't give in to pressure. Doing what you know is wrong will come back to haunt you in the end.

Not long ago, I received a letter from a girl asking if she should go to clubs with her non-Christian friends to better her relationships with them. Well, you don't have to think long to figure out that she should not be hanging around clubs for any reason. And she may need to reconsider how close she gets to those friends. There's a fine line between being exclusive and snobby in your Christianity and hanging around people who pull you down. As I quoted in the first devotional, 1 Corinthians 15:33 tells us plainly that "bad company corrupts good morals" (NASB). And 1 Corinthians 6:18 tells us to "flee immorality" (NASB). That means *run away from it!*

Be loving and kind to all people, but be careful about choosing the people you spend a lot of time with. Your closest friends should be those who encourage you to do right, not pressure you to do wrong.

Think about the kind of friend you are and examine the people you hang out with. Do you or your friends gossip about others? Are you critical of other people? Are you part of a group that excludes others? Do your friends put pressure on you to do what is wrong?

Pray for good friendships, and God will bring them to you. Just be patient. Good friends are some of the most precious treasures we can have; but bad friends are worse than no friends, and worst of all, they can pull you away from your best friend—Jesus.

STUDY GUIDE

Me and My Big Mouth

📖 **Opening Scripture:** Read Psalm 19:14. Ask God to speak to you in a specific way as you study His Word today.

❀ **What's the Big Deal about Words?** Have you ever noticed that when girlfriends get together, the words are fast and many? It seems that we just speak the first things that come into our minds without taking time to think. How many times have you said something only to feel the "pang" of regret later? It is good to have friends we feel comfortable with, but we must remember that familiarity doesn't give us the license to sin.

What's your experience? Has there ever been a time when you said something you later regretted? If so, how did you feel when you realized your mistake? _____

What were the consequences that you or someone else suffered?_____

_____

_____

❀ **Tongue Control**

What does the Word say? Read James 3:2. What does this passage say about someone who is never at fault in what he says?

❑ He is an angel.

❑ He has a bad case of laryngitis.

Me and My Big Mouth

❑ He must be a preacher.

❑ He is able to keep his whole body in check.

Think about it: This passage teaches that those who can control their mouths are able to control other areas of their lives. On the other hand, those who never learn to control their words will find they don't practice self-control in other areas.

What do you think? Why do you think we have such a hard time controlling the words we speak?

❑ Our mouths have minds of their own.

❑ We lack self-control.

❑ We talk in our sleep.

❑ We are afraid of staying silent.

What's your experience? Do you know someone who uses self-control in the way they speak to and about others? If so, describe what it is like to be around this person. _____

_____

_____

_____

✤ The Small Controls the Mighty

Fill in the blanks: Read James 3:3–12. Fill in the blanks from James 3:3: "When we put_____ into the mouths of horses to make them obey us, we can turn the _____ animal."

James 3:4: "Or take ships as an example. Although they are so large and are driven by strong winds, they are steered by a _____ _____ _____ wherever the pilot wants to go."

Think about it: Although the tongue is such a small and hidden part of the body, it can control the whole individual. It is compared to a bit that steers a horse or a rudder that directs a ship. The tongue, although it is a very small part of the body, will chart the course of your life.

What's your experience? In what ways can someone's tongue direct her life? _____

_____

Although the tongue is very small, its effects on others can be large and lasting. List some of the effects your words can have on other people. _____

_____

_____

❧ Power for Good and Evil

What does the Word say? In James 3:6, with what does the writer compare the power of the tongue?

- ❏ Flood
- ❏ Fire
- ❏ Hurricane
- ❏ Blizzard

Me and My Big Mouth

What do you think? Why do you think the Bible uses this analogy?_____

_____

Think about it: Have you ever seen a piece of land after a fire has swept through? If so, you know that there is nothing left standing. Every living thing is destroyed, whether plants, trees, or even human lives. The things people worked so hard to erect are burned down to a pile of ash. Fire is the most destructive force on earth. It has the power to destroy and kill.

How does the tongue have power to destroy and kill? _____

_____

What's your experience? Has there been a time when you used your words to destroy? If so, describe that instance. _____

_____

_____

Think about it: As you read the description about fire, you may have also remembered some of the positive uses of fire. With fire we warm our houses, cook our food, and light dark places. Just as fire has the potential to harm and destroy, it can also enhance our lives. You see, fire is a neutral force. When it is used with wisdom and caution, it helps people. But when it is used without discretion, it can kill. The power of the tongue is the same way. It can shape our destinies as well as the destinies of others. This is why it is so important to harness the power of the tongue.

List some of the ways the power of the tongue can be used for good.

_____

_____

_____

What's your experience? Describe a time when someone's words built you up._____

_____

_____

_____

❀ Our Words Reveal Our Hearts

Fill in the blanks: Read James 3:10 and fill in the missing words: "Out of the same mouth come _____ and _____. My brothers, this should not be."

What do you think? Why do you think our words sometimes honor God and at other times dishonor Him?

Fill in the blanks: Read Jesus' words in Matthew 12:34 and fill in the missing words: "For out of the overflow of the _____ the _____ speaks."

Think about it: This verse shows us the true reason our words are often less than sweet. Our words are the most accurate revelation of what is truly inside our hearts. If you are like me, this may be scary to you. All too often stinging and hurtful words reveal my heart.

Me and My Big Mouth

Thankfully, God never leaves us alone. As we yield to Him in obedience and are changed by the study of His Word, we will find that our hearts begin to change.

❧ **Inner Change:** Maybe as you have read this study, God has shown you areas where you need to change. Possibly you've seen how your words tear others down. We can destroy by the way we talk *to* others or even how we talk *about* them. The Bible refers to this kind of talk as gossip.

What does the Word say? Read Ephesians 4:29. According to this passage, does gossip fit the description for the way Christians should talk? Explain. _____

_____

_____

_____

_____

What's your experience? Are there ways you use your tongue that need to change? If so, list those. _____

_____

_____

_____

_____

Think about it: Change takes time and cooperation with the Holy Spirit, but it is possible with God's power. It may not come overnight, but it will begin as you allow God to change you from the inside out. Others may oppose your desire to change, trying to lure you into gossip or cursing, so you may need to take drastic measures in order to reject sinful patterns. This may mean you end some conversations. Others may not understand at first but will later notice the definite change in you.

✔ **Try This:** Reread the verse we read as we began our study, Psalm 19:14. Take a few minutes to write out this verse on a card or poster board. Now post it someplace you will see it each day. This may be your bathroom mirror, your locker, or even on the ceiling above your bed. Every time you see this verse, sincerely make it your prayer to God. For you see, as God changes our hearts, our words will quickly follow.

Now add these three steps to your daily routine to help you change the way you use your tongue.

1. *Prayer*—Commit to pray daily about how you use your words.
2. *Accountability*—Ask someone to pray with you and ask you regularly about your growth in this area.
3. *Awareness of His presence*—Remind yourself that even though you cannot see God, He is constantly with you, hearing your thoughts and words.

Me and My Big Mouth

✝ Living the Word

• Reread Ephesians 4:29. List the qualifications for a Christian's speech._____

_____

_____

Now describe what would happen if you went one entire day when the only words you spoke fit this description. _____

_____

_____

_____

• Read Psalm 39:1. What do you think the Bible means by putting a "muzzle" on our mouths? _____

_____

_____

_____

_____

How can you put a muzzle on your mouth to protect you from sinning in ways you have before? _____

_____

_____

_____

_____

Dear Point of Grace,

I am eighteen years old, and I just started my first year in college. I am sad and lonely, and I am having a difficult time making friends. I feel like I have to wear so many masks. I think I look happy and successful on the outside, but I feel just the opposite on the inside. It's getting hard to hide my real feelings. I have hidden them so long that I am not even sure what I feel anymore. I feel I have lost who I am. How can anyone be my friend when I don't know who I am?

Rhonda

*I praise you because I am fearfully
and wonderfully made.*
Psalm 139:14 NIV

Growing the Real You

Figuring out who *you* are may be the most challenging part of being a friend to someone else. And this means taking an honest look at yourself—looking at who you are now and who you want to become. As you work through this devotional, I really want you to believe that with God's help, you can be all He intends for you to be.

First, let's think about who you are right now. What words define and describe you? Words like . . . daughter, sister, student, dancer, brain, Christian, blonde, brunette, pretty, athletic, friend, listener, talker, moody, laid back. This list could go on and on. Take a minute right now to write down ten words that describe you. Think about your appearance, your personality, and your spiritual life.

I, _____, am

(Write your full name here.)

Friends—Terry

1. _____
2. _____
3. _____
4. _____
5. _____
6. _____
7. _____
8. _____
9. _____
10. _____

You are the only girl like you in all of the world, so don't try to be like someone else. How boring it would be if we were all alike. Just be the best *you* that you can be. God made each one of us with unique qualities that can be used for His purposes. King David said in Psalm 139:14, "I praise you because I am fearfully and wonderfully made" (NIV). Another psalm says of God: "Your hands made me and formed me" (119:73 NIV). Do you hear the message of these verses? You are "wonderfully" made, and *God* is the one who made you—on purpose! Learn to celebrate your uniqueness.

I am so glad that the four of us in Point of Grace all have different personalities. I think that is what has kept us sane over the eleven years we've been singing together. Shelley has a leader, take-charge kind of personality. Heather is laid back and passionate. Denise is energetic and outgoing, and I am organized and empathetic.

Growing the Real You

Our group has worked well *because* we are all so different. It is our four unique sets of talents and personalities that make Point of Grace the group that it is. Our theme verses could be 1 Corinthians 12:4–6, which say, "There are different kinds of gifts, but the same Spirit. There are different kinds of service, but the same Lord. There are different kinds of working, but the same God works all of them in all men" (NIV).

You are the only one just like you. Learn to relax in the good things you are. Stop comparing yourself to others. Be comfortable with your looks, your quirks, and your surroundings. You are unique. Enjoy it! Be yourself and allow others to be themselves.

Now that we've talked a little about who you are as an individual, let's tackle the difficult part of this discussion. Let's take a minute to talk about *change*. In order to be the best friend you can be—and the best person—you'll probably need to make some changes. And the kind of changes I want us to focus on are *character* changes. Character is who you are on the inside—the part of you that's still there when no one else is looking. Character qualities include things like honesty, loyalty, kindness, joy, and patience. And the good thing about character traits is that all of us can grow and develop these traits in ourselves, no matter what our personalities are like.

In a way, thinking about change is not so difficult—especially at this stage of your life. The years between ages thirteen and twenty are *full* of change. You are experiencing new emotions; you are figuring out who you are and what life is about. This time of life is filled with exciting possibilities. You can actually make a plan for who you want to become and set out to become it.

Are you the person today that you want to be ten years from now? Think about the qualities that make up a good friend—not only a good friend but also a good person—and write them below. If you'll start working on the person you want to become *now*, you can drastically affect who you will be. Here are some ideas to help you get started. A good friend is honest, forgiving, godly, encouraging, loyal, a good listener, available, giving, genuine, and fun. Also think of what a friend is not: gossipy, critical, cliquish, or out to impress others. Now list the character traits you want to have in your life. (And try not to just copy the things I listed. Think about who *you* want to be.)

I, _____, want to be:

(Write your full name here.)

1. _____
2. _____
3. _____
4. _____
5. _____
6. _____
7. _____
8. _____
9. _____
10. _____

Growing the Real You

Remember and hold on to this statement made by the apostle Paul: "I can do all things through Christ who strengthens me" (Philippians 4:13 NKJV). Choose one or two traits to work on each week, and set your mind to changing for the better. God will give you the strength to do it.

You'll be more purposeful and effective in your efforts to change if you'll write about your progress in a journal. (You could use the *Girls of Grace* journal!) Write about your daily commitment to become the person God wants you to be, and write about your struggles along the way. Remind yourself in every circumstance that you want to be a godly girl and focus on doing what is right. You can do it! Have confidence that if you have done a little thing well, you can do a bigger thing well, too.

Billy Graham, who is one of my heroes, in talking about identity crises in youth, said that the "chief symptom is the cry: 'Who am I?' To them I say, 'Have a confrontation with yourself. Then have a confrontation with Jesus Christ.'" I love that.

My dad used to tell me and my three sisters that we were beautiful on the inside, and honestly, that felt better than when he said I was beautiful on the outside. Becoming beautiful on the inside takes hard work, and when someone notices how much work you put into being a godly girl, that means the world.

Have you ever seen a woman or girl who is beautiful on the outside . . . until she opens her mouth and says something ugly? At that moment, her beauty vanishes. I have seen bitterness and jealousy eat away at outwardly beautiful people until they were actually ugly.

Friends—Terry

Last year I saw the movie *Shallow Hal*, and I wish I could see people the way Hal did. Hal's perspective about people totally changed from the beginning of the movie to the end. He had a powerful encounter with a famous speaker and was dramatically changed. Before this encounter, he judged every girl by her outward appearance; but afterward, he saw only the inner person—the heart. Some women, who were beautiful on the outside, all of a sudden were ugly and gross. He ends up falling in love with a really overweight girl because with his new perspective, he saw only her beautiful, "supermodel" heart. The poet Robert Frost said, "The only lasting beauty is the beauty of the heart." There's a lot of truth in that statement.

Lisa Ryans, in her book *For Such a Time As This*, uses the word *friendship* in place of *love* in 1 Corinthians 13:4–8 so that it reads:

Friendship is very patient and kind, never jealous or envious, never boastful or proud, never haughty or selfish or rude. Friendship does not demand its own way. It is not irritable or touchy. It does not hold a grudge and will hardly even notice when others do it wrong. If you love someone [as a friend], you will be loyal to her no matter what the cost. You will always believe in her, always expect the best of her, and always stand your ground in defending her. The love of a Godly friend...endures through every circumstance.

Remember, the inner beauty of your heart and soul will shine farther than any outer beauty ever could. Start today to become the kind of person and friend God wants you to be.

Growing the Real You

One of the girls I meet with at my church found this poem engraved on a park bench in Texas.

Some people come into our lives and quickly go.
Some people move our souls to dance;
They awaken us to a new understanding with the passing of their wisdom.
Some people make the sky more beautiful to gaze upon;
They stay in our lives for a while, leave footprints on our hearts,
And we are never, ever the same.

I want to be that to someone, don't you?

STUDY GUIDE

Am I a True Friend?

📖 **Opening Scripture:** Please begin by reading 1 Peter 3:15. Ask God to speak to you today as you study His Word.

❀ **What Is a True Friend?** What thoughts come to your mind when you hear the word *friend*? You may immediately picture someone you know who has been a faithful and caring friend. Maybe you think of characteristics demonstrated by a true friend.

What does it mean? In your own words, define the word *friend*. _____

_____

_____

_____

What do you think? In your opinion, what is the most important thing someone can do for her friend?

❑ Keep her secrets.

❑ Make memories together.

❑ Share Christ with her.

❑ Loan her money.

❀ **God's Ambassadors:** Second Corinthians 5:20 says, "We are therefore Christ's ambassadors, as though God were making his appeal through us."

Am I a True Friend?

What does it mean? The dictionary definition of an *ambassador* is "a special representative or an official agent with a special mission."

What do you think? If you are a Christian, you are sent into the world with a special mission. In what ways do you think God wants to use you to fulfill His mission in the lives of your friends? _____

_____

_____

_____

❧ **Sharing What's Truly Valuable:** Look back at your definition for the word *friend*.

What's your experience? Write about a past experience when someone offered you true friendship._____

_____

_____

If you've ever had a friend who was in need of food or money, what did you do? _____

_____

Why do you think it is so easy to share our *things* with others but so hard to share our personal relationship with Jesus?_____

_____

_____

Have you ever made an effort to share about Jesus Christ with friends? If so, how did it go? _____

_____

_____

Pray about it: If you have friends who don't personally know Jesus Christ, you can be sure God has placed them in your life so you can be a witness. Can you think of two friends who do not know Christ? If so, write their names in the following space and commit to praying for them daily: _____

_____

_____

❀ **What's Holding You Back?** If you have friends who don't know Jesus but haven't talked to them about your faith, what is holding you back?

❑ I am waiting to understand more about the Bible before I share with them.

❑ I am scared of what they will think about me.

❑ I am waiting for the best time to share with them.

❑ I know that they will reject Jesus and His love.

There are many things that hold us back from sharing His love.

1. Knowledge: Some people think they need to understand the complete truth of the Bible before they witness to others. If this were correct, no one would ever share. Not even the most eloquent preacher can fully understand the mysteries of God's Word.

God doesn't call us to know everything before we open our mouths; instead, He calls us to share what we do know with those He has placed in our lives. God used the uneducated disciples to spread His truth. He wants to use you. Are you willing? Why or why not?

_____

_____

_____

_____

2. Fear: The second excuse people use is that they are scared of what others will think about them. Have you ever used this excuse? If so, how can you overcome your fear of what others think? _____

_____

_____

_____

_____

3. Timing: Sometimes people say that they are waiting until an ideal time before they witness to someone. While this may be true, it is often just a way of putting off obedience to God. Have you ever been guilty of putting off sharing your faith with another person? If so, how can you overcome the tendency to put off obedience? _____

_____

_____

_____

4. Rejection: The last excuse people use is to claim they know the person will reject Christ. The problem with this excuse is that we cannot read another's mind. You may share with someone who looks like she has no need for Jesus but on the inside is dying to hear about Christ's love.

❀ **Preparing to Share:** Reread 1 Peter 3:15. What does this verse teach that we must do before we share?
   ❏ Become knowledgeable about the Bible
   ❏ Put Christ first in our lives
   ❏ Pray for three or four hours that God will use our words
   ❏ Understand everything our friends believe

What do you think? Why is it important that Christ is first place in our lives if we are to be effective witnesses for Him? _____

_____

_____

_____

The passage teaches that we should always be ready to share about Christ. How can you be ready at all times to share with another about your relationship with Jesus? _____

_____

Am I a True Friend?

_____

_____

❧ **A Distinct Life:** A Christian's life should be distinct enough that it stands out to unbelievers. They should wonder what is different about us. Christians should have an unusual hope that is not found in the world.

What's your experience? Does your life demonstrate to unbelievers that you have hope? If so, how? _____

_____

_____

_____

_____

What does the Word say? Read Matthew 5:14–16. Jesus compares Christians to a:

- ❏ Lighthouse
- ❏ Boat
- ❏ Bird
- ❏ Light

Think about it: We shouldn't try to draw attention to ourselves so that people will praise us for our goodness; rather, we should point them to Jesus. Our goal should be that others turn their lives over to Christ and praise our Father in heaven. Just as light in a dark room helps us find our way, we are to be the light that helps others find the way to Christ.

In what ways can you let your light shine before men? _____

_____

_____

_____

❁ Become a True Friend: Will you commit to becoming a true friend? Will you be the kind of friend who not only shares memories and secrets, but who also shares how to find eternal life through Jesus Christ? If you discovered the cure for a disease and your friend contracted that very disease, you would most certainly share the cure. As a Christian, you have the good news of forgiveness and life in Jesus Christ. Whatever you do, don't keep it to yourself!

✔ Try This: Make a list of those in your circle of friends. Next to each person's name, write something you can pray about for that person this week. Next, put a star by those who need to hear about Jesus' love. Pray over your list this week, asking God to open doors for you to share with those who do not know about Him. When the opportunities arise, take them. Don't be ashamed about what Jesus has done in your life. _____

_____

_____

Am I a True Friend?

_____

_____

✝ **Living the Word:** Read Colossians 4:5–6.

• In what ways can you be wise in the way you act toward outsiders?

_____

_____

• List some of the situations you will be in this week where unbelievers will be present. _____

_____

• What would happen if you made the most of every opportunity God gives you to share about Him this week?_____

_____

• Describe what conversation "full of grace" and "seasoned with salt" is like. _____

_____

_____

• What practical steps can you take so that your conversation fits this description? _____

_____

_____

_____

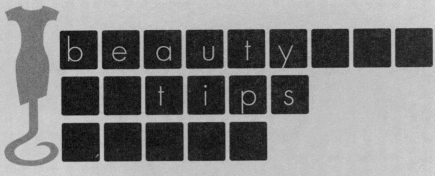

beauty tips

❀ Use cold water for a final rinse after shampooing to make hair extra shiny.

❀ Keep your hands off your face. Most zits develop by the transference of oil, dirt, and germs on your hands to your face.

❀ Never go on a "crash" diet. If you feel the need to lose weight, begin a well-balanced diet: Cut out sweets and junk food and add lots of fruits and vegetables. Choose steamed or roasted over fried. Leave off the gravy. Reduce the portions of what you eat for your three main meals and add healthy snacks in between to boost your metabolism and keep you from getting hungry.

❀ Exercise. It's great not only for the body but also for the mind. It releases stress, helps you think more clearly, gives you energy, and helps you feel better about yourself.

✿ If someone is being talked about in a gossipy way, think of something nice to say about her, then say it in a way that doesn't make the ones who are gossiping feel awkward.

✿ Don't let your eyes wander in the middle of a conversation. Make whomever you're with feel as if they have your undivided attention.

✿ Be the best secret keeper you know. The feeling of power and importance you momentarily get from showing that you are "in the know" is not as rewarding as the respect you'll get for the power you have over your tongue.

✿ Be happy when something good happens to those you don't like. You'll be surprised at how liberated you'll feel.

inner beauty tips

b♥ys

Dear Point of Grace,

I am going out with the most wonderful guy. He's so perfect for me! We like the same things like movies and music and sports, and we even have the same favorite foods and colors! But more than all that, I love the way he makes me feel that I am special—he says that nobody has ever made him feel the way I make him feel.

The only problem is that I'm afraid I've let the physical part of our relationship get out of control, and I don't know how to stop it. It's easy to be strong when I'm away from him, but as soon as we're together, I lose control. I'm a Christian, and I feel bad for doing things I shouldn't. But how can I stop now that I've gone this far? Some of my friends say that if a girl does what I've done, she isn't a virgin anymore. Should I even try to stop if my friends are right that it's too late for me, anyway?

Mary

God is so rich in mercy,
and he loved us so very much, that even while
we were dead because of our sins, he gave us life
when he raised Christ from the dead.
Ephesians 2:4–5 NLT

Our Desire for Love

The desire to be accepted and part of a group is deep within the hearts of all of us. We want to be noticed. We want to be *loved.*

But in our search for love and acceptance, we tend to look everywhere but up. God's love for us is unconditional and unending, yet we hunger for acceptance and affirmation from the people around us—especially the male version of people.

I have always liked boys. When I was two, I wanted to be a boy. When I was in kindergarten, I kissed my first boy underneath a table. But it was in junior high that I first started looking to guys for the special attention that up to then I'd found in my girlfriends, my family, and God. Until then, guys were really just good friends. I loved sports, so I loved hanging out with guys. We were buddies, and I liked it that way. But then I started noticing that all my girlfriends had boyfriends, and I began to wonder what was wrong with me. Why didn't I have a boyfriend?

In the movies, the female lead always had the cutest boyfriend. The magazines I read highlighted who was dating whom and how to find Mr. Right. My girlfriends began trying to help me find someone to "go with." The pressure to have a special someone seemed to come from everywhere. We live in a world that teaches us that "love" can be found by being the cutest, smartest, sexiest, or skinniest.

It's only natural to want the attention of the opposite sex. What girl doesn't want someone special to call her every night? Who doesn't like having someone to be giggly about at a slumber party? It's fun! When I was your age, it was much easier to get up in the morning and get ready for school when I knew I would see that cute guy in second period. Have you been there?

The problem is that in my search for attention from guys, I became distracted from my devotion to God. I lost sight of the big picture of who I was and what God wanted for me. I began to play the games that many of you play: You think a boy is cute, so you tell your best friend to tell his best friend and then somehow you end up "going out." "Going where?" my parents used to say. It would make me so mad!

After "going with" a few guys for maybe two weeks at a time, I finally got my first real boyfriend. It was the end of summer break, and I was registering for the tenth grade. This guy and I had been friends in the ninth grade, but I'll never forget seeing him in the registration line. The sparks flew! He even had his own truck, and he looked so cute driving it!

Our Desire for Love

He seemed perfect! He was a Christian, he loved God, and he was very involved with FCA (that's Fellowship of Christian Athletes). I wanted to spend every waking moment with him. We saw each other at school, church, football games, basketball games, FCA meetings—it was awesome!

But soon, the fire and passion I'd had for God in the seventh, eighth, and ninth grades became more of a flicker, and my passion for my boyfriend grew into a flame. Neither of us meant to do anything wrong. We didn't deliberately set out to disobey God. But it wasn't long before our physical relationship became less than innocent. We never "went all the way," but we did cross some lines I wish we hadn't.

I wish, now, that I had talked to someone I trusted right from the very start of our relationship—my youth minister's wife, my Sunday school teacher, even my parents. But I was too embarrassed and proud to tell them of my struggles. If I'd been honest, I know that any one of them would have helped me and saved me some regret.

Satan has a tricky way of turning down our "sin-sensitivity" level. You know what I mean. The first time you step over a line, you feel that twinge of guilt in your stomach telling you that what you're doing isn't right. But the next time you do it, you're not quite so sure of your convictions. It gets easier and easier to ignore, and pretty soon you don't feel it at all.

The Bible says that sexual sin is different from any other kind of sin: "Run away from sexual sin! No other sin so clearly affects the body as this one does. For sexual immorality is a sin against your own body" (1 Corinthians 6:18 NLT). It's different because when we share that kind of intimacy with another person, we become "one" with that person; but God wants us to be one spirit with *Him* (see 1 Corinthians 6:16–17).

God has wired us to need intimacy and love (we'll talk more about that in the next devotional), but Satan perverts that need so that we look for it in all the wrong places—and sexual intimacy outside of marriage is one of the places too many girls look.

Maybe you are one of those girls. Or maybe you've never been asked to contemplate how you act on a date. Some kids think that if they abstain from the "technical" act of sex, doing everything else is okay. This way of thinking may keep you from getting pregnant, but it isn't "okay" with God, and the spiritual and psychological damage can be just as severe as "going all the way." Studies show that Christian kids struggle with these issues just as much as non-Christians do.

But it's important to know that it's never too late to make things right— no matter what you've done in the past.

There really is no such thing as a "good girl." The Bible says that "all have sinned; all fall short of God's glorious standard" (Romans 3:23 NLT). No one— not even the most godly girl you know—can stand before God on her own merit. It is only by the grace of God, extended to us through the blood of Jesus, that we are made pure.

Did you know that the word *virgin* means "pure"? You can be pure, even now. With God's help, you can be pure in the way you think and the way you act, the way you dress and the way you carry yourself. Your relationship with guys in the future can be all new. You can be a virgin in every sense but the "technical" one.

Whether you've been looking for love in sexual relationships or in acceptance from friends or excellence in school or sports, you can turn your heart back to God and find the love you yearn for in Him.

When we trust Jesus as our sacrificial Lamb, His precious blood washes all our sins away. First John 1:7 says that when we walk in the light of Jesus, His blood cleanses us from all sin. Sin makes us feel dirty. Jesus can make us clean. Wouldn't you like to feel clean all over? A great book called *Intimate Issues* by Linda Dillow and Lorraine Pintus shares the following ideas:

Step into the shower of confession. Your "heart cleansing" starts by being open and honest with God. Tell Him every detail. Tell Him what your heart is chasing after. Confess to Him any sexual sin ("If we confess our sins, he is faithful and just and will forgive us our sins and purify us from *all unrighteousness*" 1 John 1:9 NIV). You can do this by yourself, or you can ask a special friend (not your boyfriend!) to pray with you as you confess to the Lord.

Soak in a bubble bath of His love. Sometimes this is as hard as the confession process because we don't feel we deserve God's love. We have a hard time believing that He could love us in spite of our sin. But He does. Immerse yourself in His love and accept His forgiveness. He also wants you to forgive yourself. Look at these scriptures and soak in their promises. If you struggle a lot with feeling guilty, these would be good for you to memorize: "'Their sins and lawless acts I will remember no more.' And where these have been forgiven, there is no longer any sacrifice for sin" (Hebrews 10:17–18 NIV). "'Then neither do I condemn you,' Jesus declared. 'Go now and leave your life of sin'" (John 8:11 NIV). "For I will forgive their wickedness and will remember their sins no more" (Hebrews 8:12 NIV). "Everyone who has this hope in him purifies himself, just as he is pure" (1 John 3:3 NIV). "Forget the former things; do not dwell on the past. See, I am doing a new thing! Now it springs up; do you not perceive it? I am making a way in the desert and streams in the wasteland. I, even I, am he who blots out your transgressions, for my own sake, and remembers our sins no more" (Isaiah 43:18–19, 25 NIV).

Put on some new clothes. Isaiah 61:10 says, "I am overwhelmed with joy in the LORD my God! For he has dressed me with the clothing of salvation and draped me in a robe of righteousness" (NLT). All I can say to that is "Wow!" (You might even want to buy yourself something special to celebrate your renewal—I always welcome a reason to shop.) Philippians 3:12–14 gives us hope for new beginnings: "Not that I have already obtained all this, or have already been made perfect, but I press on to take hold of that for which Christ Jesus took hold of me. Brothers, (or sisters) I do not consider myself yet to have taken hold of it. But one thing I do: Forgetting what is behind and straining toward what is ahead, I press on toward the goal to win the prize for which God has called me heavenward in Christ Jesus" (NIV).

And we can celebrate with this verse in Romans 4:7–8: "Blessed are they whose transgressions are forgiven, whose sins are covered. Blessed is the man whose sin the Lord will never count against him" (NIV).

Our Desire for Love

Now let's think back to the reason we are drawn to boys in the first place. It's because we desire to be loved. Well, we are! God loved you so much that He sent His Son to die for your sins. He did this so that you can someday be in heaven with Him and live with Him forever! If God loves you this much, don't you think He will provide for your every need? Stop trying to be God in your life. It takes a lot of pressure off.

Maybe sex is not a struggle for you. Maybe you struggle with friends, grades, clothes, or your appearance. What controls you? In a book called *Out of the Saltshaker*, Rebecca Peppert writes, "Whatever controls us is our lord. The person who seeks power is controlled by power. The person who seeks acceptance is controlled by acceptance. We do not control ourselves. We are controlled by the lord of our lives."

Make sure that you are looking for love in the right place. Make sure that Jesus is the Lord of your life. I encourage you to sit down and think about what is most important to you. Talk to God about it. Ask Him to help you make Him first in your life. For me, it's not something I can do once. It's a daily effort of seeking Him. The good news is that He is always pursuing you—and He will never stop.

My First Love

📖 **Opening Scripture:** Begin by reading Matthew 22:36–38. This may be a familiar passage to you, so ask God to give you a heart to hear from Him in a new way today.

❀ **First Love:** We have all dreamed about someday falling in love. We read about it in books and see it in movies. We anticipate the day we'll meet someone special and our lives will never be the same.

Think about it: What do you look forward to the most about falling in love someday? _____

_____

_____

Did you know that God wants to be the very first love of your life, before any other person? How does that make you feel?_____

_____

Does it make you feel incredibly valued and special? It should. The God of the entire universe desires for you to love Him first. What an amazing thought.

❀ **He Wants *All* of You:** How can we make God our first love? Let's look at Matthew 22:37 again to find out.

Fill in the blanks: "Jesus replied: 'Love the Lord your God with _____ your heart and with _____ your soul and with _____ your mind.'"

My First Love

Think about it: The key word here is *all*. God isn't content for us to bring Him the leftover parts of ourselves after we've given our love elsewhere. He wants to be our first love.

The first part of the verse talks about loving the Lord with all your heart. This means we must guard against giving first place to anyone other than God. Only He should occupy first place.

Take some time to think about your own heart. What person or thing has first place right now?
- ❏ My family and friends
- ❏ Finding happiness for myself
- ❏ God
- ❏ Other: _____.

❀ All of Your Heart

Think about it: If God isn't the first love in your heart right now, what are some practical steps you can take to change that? _____

_____

_____

_____

What does the Word say? Read Psalm 73:25–26.

Have you ever stumbled upon a love letter or e-mail that was very personal and private? In a sense, Psalm 73 is a love letter in which Asaph, the writer, pours his heart out to God.

What is the writer saying to God in this psalm?

❏ "God, I know You aren't in first place now, but someday You will be."

❏ "God, please help me to get out of the mess I am in."

❏ "God, You fill my heart in a way that no one else can."

❏ "God, help me to understand You more."

Fill in the blanks: Read Psalm 73:26 and fill in the missing words. "My flesh and my heart may fail, but God is the _____ of my heart and my _____ forever."

What do you think? What do you think the writer means by "My flesh and my heart may fail"? _____

_____

What is meant by the phrase "strength of my heart"? _____

_____

What's your experience? Has there ever been a time when you found the strength of your heart in God? If so, describe that experience._____

_____

_____

Think about it: Every word matters in a love letter. The writer chooses words that hold special meaning. In using the word *portion*, Asaph simply means that God satisfies Him. In a sense it is like when you are satisfied by a hearty meal; you are completely full, not wanting for more.

My First Love

Can you honestly make the same declaration as the psalmist, that your relationship with God satisfies you in a way no other relationship does? Explain your answer. _____

_____

_____

_____

_____

_____

✿ All of Your Soul

Think about it: In Matthew 22:37, Jesus also calls us to love God with all of our souls. Your soul is the part of you made up of will and emotions. It determines your behavior. Knowing this, why is it so important that we love God with our souls? _____

_____

_____

_____

_____

Fill in the blanks: Read Colossians 1:16 and fill in the missing words. "For by him all things were created: things in heaven and on earth, visible and invisible, whether thrones or powers or rulers or authorities; _____ _____ were created _____ him and _____ him."

What does the Word say? Now look closely at the last part of the verse. Why were all things created?

- ❑ Because God needed to spend some time on something, so why not creating?
- ❑ For Him
- ❑ For there to be something to study in history class
- ❑ For the beauty of the earth

According to this verse, what was God's purpose in creating you?

_____

_____

_____

What's your experience? In what ways can you choose to live *for Him*?

_____

_____

_____

❁ All of Your Mind

Think about it: In Matthew 22:37, Jesus calls us to love Him with all of our minds. We often think of love in terms of our heart or choices, while we rarely think of it as an act of our minds.

What does the Word say? Let's read Exodus 20:4–5 and see what we can learn. This passage comes straight from the Ten Commandments. God tells His people He is jealous for them. He commands them to worship no other person or thing. God doesn't want thoughts about others to occupy greater space in our minds than our thoughts about Him.

What's your experience? In what ways have you been guilty of placing others ahead of God in your mind? _____

_____

Think about it: One way we do this is by allowing our thoughts to be captivated by another person or thing. We must guard what we allow into our minds because wrong thoughts can eventually become strongholds over us.

In what ways can you guard the things you allow into your mind?

_____

_____

❖ **Only God Can Meet Your Deepest Needs:** God created us with needs for love, acceptance, and security, but we must allow Him to meet those primary needs before going to anyone else. No human love can fill up those empty places inside of you. You must never allow yourself to believe someone else can meet needs only God can meet.

What's your experience? Has there ever been a time when you looked to someone else to meet needs that only God could meet? If so, what happened? _____

_____

_____

_____

✔ **Try This:** Take a few moments to examine the loves of your heart today. Will you commit to love God with all your heart, soul, and mind? If so, every other love will be put in its proper place. Are there some changes you need to make? If so, what action steps are you going to take to make those a reality?_____

_____

_____

_____

_____

_____

✟ **Living the Word:** Reread Psalm 73:25–26.

• The writer has a strong appetite for intimacy with God. He says his desire for God surpasses all other desires. What about you? Do your appetites for other things surpass your appetite for God? If so, what changes will you make? _____

_____

_____

_____

_____

My First Love

_____

_____

• Other people may love you fully, but only God can love you perfectly. God is the only One who will never fail you. Write a prayer of thanksgiving to Him. You may want to get ideas from Psalm 73 for your love letter to Him. _____

_____

_____

_____

_____

_____

_____

Dear Point of Grace,

I heard something the other day about how Christians my age shouldn't date until they're ready to get married— that they should "court" instead. I really want to do what's right, but I've been going out with boys ever since sixth grade, and dating doesn't seem like such a serious deal as they're trying to make it out to be. I don't have a boyfriend at the moment, and I feel kinda left out without one. Plus, I'm afraid that I won't have a date to the prom (which is what I really want!).

Sometimes I think I might be happy just hanging with my guy friends, but some of them want to be "friends with benefits" (you know, where you just kiss for fun), so I might as well have a boyfriend. What do you think?

Stephanie

So whether you eat or drink or
whatever you do,
do it all for the glory of God.
1 Corinthians 10:31 NIV

The Dating Dilemma

Dating has become quite *the* discussion in Christian circles. Should people date? Or should they court? What about holding hands or kissing? What's right? What's wrong? What difference does it all make?

When I first heard about the book by Joshua Harris called *I Kissed Dating Goodbye*, my first reaction was, "This is a little extreme, don't ya think?" However, after reading it and the author's next book, *Boy Meets Girl*, I have some different thoughts on the subject.

I realized that what really matters is not whether we date or court—what really matters is, *Are we listening to God? Are we glorifying Him in our relationships?* This main issue is not even boy-girl relationships—it's more about how we love and respect others—all others—not just boys. The real question is, *Do I encourage those I know to love and trust God more?*

Boys—Denise

As I think back over the guys I dated in high school and college, I realize that that question didn't even enter my mind. I never asked, "Lord, how can a relationship with this guy draw me closer to You, and how can I show him how great You are?" Josh Harris says that if we *really* care for someone, we would think about what's best for his relationship with Christ. If we would put on the mind of Christ in any relationship, imagine how much more we would care for others!

Now, I'm not encouraging "missionary dating" (that's dating someone who is not a Christian in hopes of bringing them to Christ). In fact, I highly advise against dating a non-Christian. Sure, every now and then a non-Christian guy will come to know the Lord while dating a Christian girl, but the odds are *very* low.

You need to know that it is not your responsibility to make your boyfriend walk obediently with God. I often thought that I was the moral police for the guys I dated. But in reality, the guys you date are responsible for making their own choices. If you don't agree with those choices, then maybe you should rethink the relationship. You don't have to be judgmental, but some of their wrong choices can affect you and drag you down. In those cases, it might be better just to be friends.

High school can be such a fun part of life, so why does dating have to complicate everything so much? It goes back to the issue of what we are searching for and who we find our security in. The problem is that being intimate (like kissing, hugging, holding hands, and a lot more) has become so common with people your age that it seems odd when that's not part of a relationship. Is there something wrong with just being great friends? Can't you still go out to movies, football games, and concerts? We often think we have to do more.

Whether you decide to date or not, it's important to listen to God's voice. As I sat with a group of girls in my living room recently, I asked them what they thought about dating and courting. Most of them still wanted to date. So, if that is the case with you, there are several good guidelines to help you through the dating process. One excellent book is *I Gave Dating a Chance* by Jeramy Clark. I'd also like to share the following ideas:

Pray about it. What's the first thing you should do if there's a particular guy you want to get to know better? When I was a teen, the first thing I did was try to be around the guy and flirt to make him notice me. But I was wrong. The first thing I should have done was pray about it and tell God how I felt.

Examine your motives. The next thing I should have done was ask myself why I wanted to be with the guy so much. Did I want to date him just to make myself look good? Was I feeling left out and just wanted *someone* to date so I'd fit in with everyone else? Even if he's a really neat Christian guy and you have a lot in common, make sure that your motives are right. And remember, you don't have to date a guy to have him as a friend. Many of the best guy-girl relationships are *friendships*.

Trust God with your future. Why do we find it so hard to trust God with our future? I remember having my life all mapped out in high school—the marriage, the kids, the kind of jobs we would have. I was in the eleventh grade! I had no idea what path God would take me on during the next ten years. Why did I feel like it was so important to know all this stuff? Think about it—how often do we try to *make* things happen? We try to be matchmakers instead of letting the Maker make the match. (Girls are the worst about this!) I remember walking by the gym about the time I knew practice was over just so I could run into a certain guy "by chance." We were always trying to push our guy friends into telling us whom they asked to the prom. We are *so nosy!* We are the ones forcing guys to ask girls out. If we left them alone, many relationships would probably never start, and fewer people would end up getting hurt by breakups.

Be accountable to others. Okay. Let's say you've checked your motives and you think you're on track. Now let's say that he asks you out. What do you do next? Well, after you climb off the ceiling and call your girlfriends, you really need to stop and pray about it again. Talk to people other than just your girlfriends— like your parents, Sunday school teacher, or youth minister. See what they think, and if it all seems right, then say "yes," but make sure you proceed with caution. Set boundaries and plan ahead. You can't wait until you're with a guy in a parked car somewhere to decide that it's not a good thing.

Get your parents involved in some of these decisions. If they don't set a curfew, make a reasonable one for yourself. Talk to them and share your heart about having a godly relationship. There is no one on earth I would rather not disappoint than my parents. If you are blessed with godly parents, welcome it. But even if they're not Christian parents, most of them want you to have boundaries and dating guidelines because they love you.

It's good to have an accountability relationship with your godly girlfriends. I know a precious girl who is part of an accountability group. They pray for each other before dates and call each other with the details after the date. (If you do this, make sure your conversation doesn't become a gossip session.) If you're in junior high or high school, I also suggest you share the details of your date with an adult. When you know you're going to give an honest report to someone, you are less likely to stray from your principles. I wish I'd had someone to share my struggles with—it would have changed a lot of things for me.

Know the limits. A question that is asked a lot is, *How far is too far?* When you ask this question, make sure you're not just wanting to know how much you can get away with. I can't refer you to a verse in the Bible that says holding hands or kissing is wrong, but I do know this—God puts a conscience in each one of us, and His Holy Spirit "speaks" to us. Even kissing can be too intimate in some relationships. I also know that when we go too far, our sinful nature tends to tune out the Holy Spirit's warnings. That is why it is so important to set guidelines before you ever get into a relationship.

Don't "waste" your time on useless dates. Now, I don't mean this in a snobbish way—I mean it in a wise, prayerful way. As I look back at my dating years—especially in college—I see so many useless dates. They didn't benefit me or the guy I went out with. I was just dating to date. Many of these guys might have been fine friends, but dating them just complicated things. Make sure the relationship is "worth" the time and effort.

Be careful about praying together. Here's a heads-up: Praying alone with a guy you're dating is usually not a good idea—unless maybe it's a quick simple prayer to set the tone at the beginning of a date. Prayer is one of the most intimate of communications and can bring out all sorts of emotions.

Sometimes being spiritually intimate can lead to physical intimacy. You absolutely should pray *for* each other, but aside from a brief "before-the-date" prayer, you should do it separately or in the presence of a man or woman you respect.

Avoid influences that "stir you up" sexually. Be careful about the movies and TV shows you watch, about the music you listen to, the books you read, and the people you hang around with. All of these things can influence your thinking and tempt you to respond sinfully.

The New Living Translation of Romans 6:12–13 says this: "Do not let sin control the way you live; do not give in to its lustful desires. Do not let any part of your body become a tool of wickedness, to be used for sinning. Instead, give yourselves completely to God since you have been given new life. And use your whole body as a tool to do what is right for the glory of God."

Because we are saved, we are no longer slaves to sin. By God's grace through what Jesus did for us on the cross, we no longer have sin *ruling* over us. But unfortunately, that does not mean that sin no longer has an *influence* in our lives. That is why it's necessary to know God by reading His Word every day and surrounding ourselves with godly people. Don't place yourself in situations that you know have a strong chance for a bad outcome.

In thinking about all we've discussed, remember to always ask yourself, "Am I glorifying God in this relationship?" "Am I as concerned about my friend or boyfriend as I am about myself?" The reason we are here on earth is to glorify and have fellowship with God and shine His light into the lives of those around us. Remember, dating isn't just about dating—

it's about looking at how we can include God in the things we do and the people we interact with.

I challenge you to take some time to evaluate the special relationships in your life. Ask God to show you how you have or haven't shown His glory through your relationships. Even though I was imperfect in many of my dating relationships, and even though I still fail my friends, my husband, and my children from time to time today; I'm thankful that God loves me perfectly and that one day we, too, will love perfectly.

STUDY
GUIDE

Safety in Standards

📖 **Opening Scripture:** Start by praying that God would give you ears to hear and obey Him today as you study His Word. Now read Psalm 119:9.

Fill in the blanks: "How can a young man keep his way _____? By living according to your _____."

❧ **God's Word—Your Guide to Purity:** Psalm 119:9 could also apply to a "young woman." You may have asked yourself the same question that the verse asks: "How can I stay pure in this world?" It seems that walking in purity gets harder each year. Temptation seems to come from everywhere. Isn't it amazing how God's Word applies to our lives today? The questions asked thousands of years ago are still around. So are the answers; they are found in God's Word.

What does the Word say? The answer to the question is in the second part of the verse. What is it?
- ❏ If we try hard, we can remain pure.
- ❏ The only way to stay pure is to lock yourself in your room.
- ❏ We can stay pure if we stay in God's Word.
- ❏ Purity is impossible, so we should just stop trying.

Think about it: Those who walk in purity live according to the teachings and principles of God's Word. They take the Word of God seriously by learning and applying it to their lives.

Safety in Standards

What part does the Bible play in determining your behavior?

❏ The Bible has little to do with my daily life.

❏ I am growing more each day in applying God's Word to my life.

❏ I have little interest in learning more about the Bible.

❏ God's Word hasn't been a big part of my life in the past, but I want to change that.

What do you think? Why is the Bible critical if we want to live in purity?

_____

_____

_____

Think about it: The Bible is God's handbook for life. He made you for Himself and has graciously provided you His owner's manual, the Bible, to teach you how to live. In that manual, He includes instructions for every area of life. There are teachings regarding family, money, life purpose, and even love. Those who are wise read and obey His Word. They save themselves from unnecessary consequences and heartache.

❧ **The Blessings of Boundaries:** God's Word provides us boundaries for living. Although boundaries may seem inconvenient, they really save lives. If it weren't for boundaries, people would walk off of ledges or drive off dangerous roads. Have you ever been to the Grand Canyon? Everywhere you look there are railings that serve as boundaries to hold people back from the dangerous edge. They are there for safety.

What's your experience? Can you think of a boundary that has kept you safe? It may be a rule your parents have set or a principle from the Bible. List it here. _____

_____

Think about it: Setting boundaries in your dating life will protect you. Boundaries are simply decisions you make before you find yourself in a particular situation. _____

_____

What's your experience? Have you ever determined boundaries for your dating life? If so, what are they? If not, why not? _____

_____

❧ The Bible's Guidelines for Dating

1. Date Christian boys.

Fill in the blanks: Read 2 Corinthians 6:14 and fill in the missing words: "Do not be _____ together with _____. For what do _____ and wickedness have in _____? Or what fellowship can light have with _____?"

Think about it: A "yoke" joins together two oxen for the purpose of doing a particular job, such as plowing a field. The writer is using this word picture to teach that Christians must only be joined to other Christians. If you are a Christian, the only guys you should ever consider dating are other growing Christians who can challenge you in your relationship with Christ.

What do you think? What is your response to this statement?

- ❑ I want to obey God in every part of life, so I will follow this principle.
- ❑ That is crazy! Who would I date?
- ❑ I have not done this in the past, but I am willing to change.
- ❑ This will mean a radical life change for me, but I choose obedience over my own desires.

2. Trust God.

Think about it: You may be thinking, *Great, that means I have only three options for guys to date.* Although you may not know many Christian guys now, that doesn't mean that you will never meet any. God will bring the right person into your life when He is ready. Will you trust Him by walking according to His standards?

What does the Word say? Read Proverbs 3:5–6. Why do you think we are told to lean not on our own understanding? _____

_____

What's your experience? What practical steps can you take to acknowledge Him in all your ways when it applies to your dating life?

_____

_____

What do you think? According to this passage, what is the benefit of trusting and acknowledging God? _____

_____

_____

The more we trust in God's goodness, the easier it is to wait for His timing. Why do you think this is true? _____

_____

3. Avoid sexual immorality.

What does the Word say? Read 1 Thessalonians 4:3–5. If you are looking for God's will, He states it in this passage. What is His will for you? _____

_____

Think about it: In what ways could you avoid sexual immorality?_____

_____

_____

The Bible is clear that any sexual activity before marriage is sin. We are not to draw a line and see how close we can come to that line; instead, we must stay as far away from sinful behavior as possible. This means we should avoid all tempting situations.

Safety in Standards

What do you think? What are some boundaries you can set now that will help you avoid tempting situations later? _____

_____

_____

_____

✔ **Try This:** Take some time to think about the boundaries you will set for your dating life. Remember, good boundaries always line up with the Word of God. You may decide you won't be alone with a guy. If you don't have a "curfew," you might want to set one for yourself—and honor it. The more decisions you make to protect your purity, the easier it will be. On a date is not the time to determine your boundaries. They need to be decided long before your date picks you up. Boundaries may seem limiting now, but the rewards they bring are limitless.

Write your list of boundaries down and place them where you will see them often. Next, share them with a parent or trusted adult and ask that person to hold you accountable for living according to those standards.

✟ **Living the Word:** In order to stay pure, you must know how to battle temptation. Some think they can overcome it with sheer will power, while others say victory is impossible.

• Read 1 Corinthians 10:12–13 to see what God's Word says about temptation.

What warning is given in verse 12? _____

_____

_____

How can you apply this verse to your dating life? _____

_____

_____

_____

• We are all tempted at times, but the true test of someone who walks with God is how she responds to temptation. Verse 13 says that God provides a "way out" from temptation.

What do you think this phrase means? _____

_____

_____

_____

• Have you ever been in a tempting situation and taken the way out? If so, describe that experience. _____

_____

_____

_____

_____

Safety in Standards

If not, what will you do differently the next time? _____

_____

_____

_____

_____

_____

Dear Point of Grace,

The other day somebody from school asked me if I was still a virgin in a way that made me feel bad for being one. My parents tell me all the time that waiting for marriage is what God wants me to do, but they aren't my age, and they have no clue what I have to go through each day. I have a boyfriend, and he and I have kissed, but that's all. There have been a few times when both of us wanted to do more than kiss, but I just didn't feel right about it, so we stopped.

But I'm so confused! Everything on TV seems to say that it's OK to have sex before marriage, and it's like people don't even think anything is wrong with sex before marriage. My body is telling me one thing, but my mind and my heart are trying to say something else. How can I have these feelings and still wait until I'm married?

Amy

*For this reason a man will leave
his father and mother and be united to his wife,
and they will become one flesh.*
Genesis 2:24 NIV

Sex as God Designed It

Do you remember the first time you learned about sex? I imagine that many of you learned about it earlier than I did. I saw "those films" in the fifth grade that talked about sex and about the whole menstrual cycle. My mother also had "the talk" with me around that same time. It was fairly vague, and I remember thinking, *Ugh! I don't want to hear this from my mother!* It all seemed rather gross.

I also remember being at a conference for teens when I was thirteen. The speaker talked about French kissing and touching, and I leaned over and said to my best friend, "I will *never* do that!" However, as my hormone levels started to change, the other gender began to look rather interesting. Why? Because God created men and women to come together as husband and wife and to become one flesh.

The First Love Story. Genesis 2 records the account of the first man and woman ever in the world. It's really a beautiful story. Take a minute to read it. If you've read it before, try to read it fresh and imagine what it must have been like for them.

> The LORD God took the man and put him in the Garden of Eden to work it and take care of it....
>
> The LORD God said, "It is not good for the man to be alone. I will make a helper suitable for him."
>
> Now the LORD God had formed out of the ground all the beasts of the field and all the birds of the air. He brought them to the man to see what he would name them; and whatever the man called each living creature, that was its name. So the man gave names to all the livestock, the birds of the air and all the beasts of the field.
>
> But for Adam no suitable helper was found. So the LORD God caused the man to fall into a deep sleep; and while he was sleeping, he took one of the man's ribs and closed up the place with flesh. Then the LORD God made a woman from the rib he had taken out of the man, and he brought her to the man.
>
> The man said, "This is now bone of my bones and flesh of my flesh; she shall be called 'woman,' for she was taken out of man." For this reason a man will leave his father and mother and be united to his wife, and they will become one flesh.
>
> The man and his wife were both naked, and they felt no shame. (verses 15, 18–25 NIV)

Isn't that a beautiful love story? Can you imagine the wonder they felt as they first discovered each other? And notice that man was not complete until woman was created. Ah…we are special, indeed. The New American Standard Bible says in verse 22 that we were "fashioned" from Adam's rib. No wonder we like shopping so much; we were in "fashion" from the very beginning.

God made man from the dust of the ground, but He chose to make woman from the man's bone and flesh to symbolize that they were one flesh. The fact that we females were created from man does a lot to explain why we yearn to be in relationship with the opposite sex. Men and women are linked in a very special way. God said that men and women, when they are united together, actually become one flesh.

The Mystery of Married Love. So you see, sex was God's idea. God has given us a beautiful gift in sex, but He firmly restricts it to marriage. The Book of Ephesians gives us an amazing insight into marriage: it tells us that marriage symbolizes Christ's relationship with His church. Ephesians 5:31 quotes Genesis 2:24 ("For this reason a man will leave his father and mother and be united to his wife, and the two will become one flesh" NIV), then goes on to say, "This is a great mystery, but it is an illustration of the way Christ and the church are one" (verse 32 NLT).

God's plan is that sex in marriage show us a picture of what our relationship with Him can be—perfect oneness. He made man and woman a perfect fit so that when they come together there is nothing between them. God wants our relationship with Him to be like that.

In the book *Mystery of Marriage*, Mike Mason says, "For in touching a person of the opposite sex in the most secret place of his or her body, with one's own most private part, there is something that reaches beyond touch, that gets behind flesh itself to the place where it connects with spirit." So you see, physical intimacy is more than skin deep; it connects us on a spiritual level—a level that is reserved only for marriage.

Genesis 2:25 says that they were both naked and felt no shame. Oh my, did I say "naked"? Isn't that a bad thing? It wasn't supposed to be. Not in God's creation. You see, before man and woman sinned, everything was perfect. They weren't just physically naked, but their hearts and souls were also open to each other as well. Communication, openness, and honesty were not problems. God designed marriage to help fulfill our needs for intimacy and closeness.

Perfection Spoiled. But things didn't stay perfect for long. After Adam and Eve sinned, things began to change. They blamed each other. They hid from God because they were embarrassed of their nakedness.

And after that, things went from bad to worse. In the New Testament, the apostle Paul said, "They knew God, but they wouldn't worship Him as God or even give Him thanks. And they began to think up foolish ideas of what God was like. The result was that their minds became dark and confused. So God let them go ahead and do whatever shameful things their hearts desired. As a result, they did vile and degrading things with each other's bodies" (Romans 1:21, 24 NLT).

Sex as God Designed It

Sound familiar? Isn't that what much of America is doing? No wonder we get so confused about sex.

Confusing Messages about Sex. So, if sex is from God, why do we often think of it as dirty or nasty? Unfortunately, our world has taken one of the most beautiful parts of God's creation and misused it for selfish reasons. There are so many different views about sex that it can be rather confusing. Plus, many of the ideas are so conflicting that it really makes it hard to figure it all out. Here are some different views that I'm aware of. Do any seem familiar to you? "Everyone is doing it." "Only bad girls enjoy sex." "Honey, just wait till you've been married twenty years. It gets *old*!" "A truly 'sexy' girl will get turned on instantly." "Boys and girls are naturally perfect lovers. They know exactly what to do." "Kisses are always perfect and romantic."

Or, worse, you may hear *nothing at all*. It's no wonder we don't know what to think.

I am sorry that some adults downplay or talk bad about sex in their marriages, because it's awesome and should be enjoyed. Maybe one reason that sex outside of marriage seems so exciting is that the unmarried are the only ones talking about it. (I'm not saying that people should share their juicy details, but it would be nice to hear how much fun marriage is.)

"Fix your thoughts on what is true and honorable and right. Think about things that are pure and lovely and admirable. Think about things that are excellent and worthy of praise" (Philippians 4:8 NLT). Let's stop thinking about sex as something that is forbidden and naughty and start thinking about how awesome it will be someday when you've waited for a godly man and for your wedding night.

A Steamy Love Story. There is a book in the Bible that can compete with any romance novel you could ever read. However, you rarely hear sermons or talks about this book. I think it's because we are embarrassed to talk about the beauty of "sex" in church. Instead, we hear, "Don't do it. It's forbidden." I believe that God put this book in His Word for a purpose. The Song of Solomon is a descriptive story about the love between a man and a woman.

Solomon says to his future bride, "You are a garden locked up, my sister, my bride; you are a spring enclosed, a sealed fountain" (Song of Songs 4:12 NIV). He found her especially beautiful because no one else had trespassed in her garden. It had been saved for him to enjoy. He delighted in her love: "Your love is more delightful than wine" (1:2 NIV).

Love and sex are supposed to be delightful. God wants us to find that one person about whom we can say, "My lover is mine and I am his" (Song of Songs 2:16 NIV). And that person is to know you like no one else knows you. My precious husband, Stu, knows my deepest secrets. He not only knows what makes me laugh or cry, but he has seen and done things with me that no one else has. It's a bond that is right. Don't spoil the intimacy you are to have with your husband alone by sharing it with someone else.

We are also warned several times in Song of Solomon "not to awaken love until the time is right" (2:7, 3:5, 8:4 NLT). These verses remind us that in a time of weakness you can spoil the beautiful relationship God has prepared for you. You are so special and so unique. Don't give away and mess up what God created for you to enjoy.

True Love. What is true love anyway? First Corinthians 13:4–7 tells us exactly what love is like: "Love is patient and kind. Love is not jealous or boastful or proud or rude. Love does not demand its own way. Love is not irritable, and it keeps no record of when it has been wronged. It is never glad about injustice but rejoices whenever the truth wins out. Love never gives up, never loses faith, is always hopeful, and endures through every circumstance" (NLT).

Examine any relationship you now have or may have in the future in light of this definition of love. If you are truly in love, you will be "patient," as Scripture says, and wait for God and His timing. If your boyfriend loves you, he will not pressure you, and he will wait, too. If he pressures you and is not patient in his love for you, then maybe he is not the one for you.

Remember that "Love does not demand its own way." Isn't "making out" all about getting your or his own way? And true love "rejoices whenever truth wins out." The truth is that God loves you more than you can ever understand. He knows the very best for you.

Just the other day, as I told my son Price—for the fifty millionth time—to stop trying to climb into the fireplace, I thought, *Why do I continually tell him that?* It was an easy question to answer: Because I love him and know that he could get burned. Why do you think God continually warns us about sex outside of marriage? Because He knows how dangerous it is. Let's stop playing with fire. Okay?

Worth the Wait. Your time will come if you will just hold out. I promise it will be worth the wait. All four of us waited until we were married to have sex. If we were able to wait, so can you! I honestly believe that one of the reasons so many marriages break up is that more and more couples have sex before they get married, and they later wonder whether they were ever truly in love or if their attraction was purely physical.

I'll never forget hearing Heather talk about her spiritual struggles before she met Brian. She was going through a difficult time of questioning. The three of us were happily married, and she didn't even have a prospect. One day, on her knees, crying out to the Lord, she finally came to the realization that God wanted some special time with just her. She made the choice to focus on and nurture her relationship with Him. And, of course, not too soon after that, Brian came into the picture.

I'm often amazed at how God works. Look back to Adam and Eve. "For Adam no suitable helper was found." But God had a plan all along. God put Adam into a deep sleep and gave him the perfect mate. I am just as guilty as you may be of trying to make things happen instead of trusting the Lord and waiting on Him. It's not always easy to wait—I know Heather would testify to that. But she would also testify that God was right in the end.

Your Wedding Night

📖 **Opening Scripture:** Please begin by reading James 1:17. Ask God to teach you from His Word today.

❀ **Sex—A Gift from God:** You have probably dreamed about your wedding day a thousand times. Most girls love to plan and envision what that day will be like. What kind of dress will you wear? What will your cake look like? How many bridesmaids will you have? If you are like most girls, you will change your mind a hundred times before that day arrives.

For all the dreaming about your wedding day, how often have you dreamed about your wedding night? Did you know that God designed that night to be like no other in your life? He planned for the wedding night between a man and woman to be like a gift they unwrap from one another. He planned for sex to be that gift.

Fill in the blanks: Fill in the missing words from James 1:17: "Every _____ and _____ gift is from above, coming down from the Father of heavenly lights, who does not change like shifting shadows."

What's your experience? Do you like gifts? If you're like most people, you love to receive gifts, both large and small. Who doesn't like to unwrap a pretty package to see what surprise is waiting for her?

Your Wedding Night

What is the best gift you ever received and why? _____

_____

_____

_____

_____

_____

Think about it: While earthly gifts are fun and brighten our days, they in no way compare to the kind of gifts God gives. His gifts surpass our wildest imaginations. They're what we would have asked for if we would have known what to ask for. He made us, so He knows the exact gift that will bring us the most joy.

Sex is a gift from God. He created it for a bride and groom to unwrap on their wedding night and not a day before.

Pray about it: Ask God to help you remember that His ways are always best and His gifts are perfect.

❧ Sex Outside of Marriage

Fill in the blanks: Read Hebrews 13:4 and fill in the missing words: "Marriage should be _____ by all, and the marriage_____ kept _____, for God will judge the adulterer and all the _____ immoral."

What do you think? According to this verse, how serious is the sin of sex before marriage?

Boys—Study Guide

❏ God really doesn't care as long as people love each other.

❏ God takes it very seriously and judges those who disobey Him.

❏ God understands that times have changed and allows people to make their own rules.

❏ God isn't concerned about this area of my life.

Think about it: This passage is one of many that deals with sexual immorality. The term "the marriage bed" refers to sexual activity. The Bible is explicitly clear about the matter. We are to wait until marriage before we have sex.

Abstinence until marriage is not a popular decision in our culture. The word *virgin* is laughed at on TV and in the movies. Those committed to purity are constantly pressured to change their decision.

What's your experience? Has there ever been a time when you were laughed at or pressured because of your commitment to stay sexually pure? If so, how did that experience make you feel? _____

_____

_____

_____

❂ Consequences of Sexual Sin

Fill in the blanks: Read Proverbs 6:32 and fill in the missing words: "But a man who commits adultery lacks_____; whoever does so _____ himself."

Your Wedding Night

What do you think? What are some ways that sexual sin can cause one to destroy herself? _____

_____

_____

Think about it: The consequences for sexual sin are devastating. You may know someone who has become pregnant or contracted a sexually transmitted disease. Often the most serious consequences are the unseen scars on the heart. This isn't to say God can't forgive someone; He will forgive her, but He doesn't remove the consequences of sin.

❁ Commit to Purity

Think about it: Will you commit to remaining sexually pure? If so, what are some practical steps you can take to make sure you wait? _____

_____

_____

It may not be the easiest decision you make, but it is well worth it. You may want to take offensive measures that will strengthen you to overcome temptation. The big decision to wait until marriage is reinforced by the many little decisions you make from day to day.

What do you think? List some benefits of sexual purity. _____

_____

_____

_____

_____

What's your experience? One important offensive step is to avoid tempting situations. If you do find yourself in a situation where you are being tempted, do you leave immediately? Why or why not? ____

_____

_____

_____

_____

_____

❀ Guard Your Heart

What does the Word say? Read Proverbs 4:23. What command does God give us in this passage? _____

_____

What do you think? What are some practical ways that you can do this?
- ❏ Wear a shield over my heart.
- ❏ Be careful about the things that I allow to influence me.
- ❏ Don't watch any TV at all.
- ❏ Bury all of my romantic feelings.

Think about it: Have you ever noticed how girls are careful in so many areas of life but absolutely careless when it comes to their hearts? God knows that our hearts are fragile, so He warns us to guard them.

Your Wedding Night

What's your experience? How seriously do you take the command to guard your heart?

- ❏ I have been careless in the past, but I am going to change after today.
- ❏ Because I have been hurt in the past, I now know that I must take it seriously.
- ❏ I have been cautious, knowing that my heart is fragile and easily broken.
- ❏ The more I grow in Christ, the more I am growing in this area.

Pray about it: Ask God to help you guard your heart as you wait for Him to bring your husband to you one day. How specifically will you ask Him to help you? _____

_____

_____

✔ **Try This:** Find the prettiest piece of paper you have. Now go to a place where you can be alone for a while. Write a letter to your future husband. You may want to tell him what you are feeling and thinking right now. Tell him that you are committed to staying sexually pure from this day on. Share with him your desire to give him the gift of your purity on your wedding night. After you finish the letter, date it and seal it in an envelope. Now put it in a safe place. Save that letter until your wedding night when you give it to your husband.

✝ Living the Word

• What if you have already participated in sexual activity? Are you exempt from God's blessings? Absolutely not. God offers His forgiveness to those who ask Him.

• Read I John 1:9. What promise does God give us if we confess our sins to Him? _____

_____

• This passage doesn't say that He might forgive us, but rather that He will. Will you claim this promise and choose to believe Him? If so, write a prayer thanking Him for His forgiveness. _____

_____

_____

_____

• He promises to purify us from all unrighteousness. First John 1:9 doesn't say "some" unrighteousness, but "all." That means that when He forgives us, He forgives completely. We are made pure again.

• Will you ask Him to forgive you today? He longs to restore you and to strengthen you to walk in purity from this day forward.

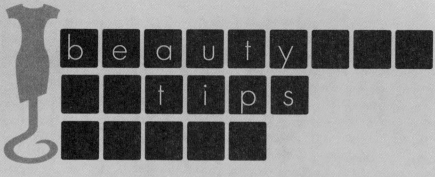

beauty tips

❀ Drink eight glasses of water every day. It helps your skin and keeps you healthy. Fill eight eight-ounce (or four sixteen-ounce) bottles of water each day, and when you drink them all—you're done!

❀ Don't try to squeeze your body into clothes that are too small. Tight clothes only emphasize figure problems. Wear clothes that fit, and you'll be amazed by how great you can look.

❀ Makeup only looks as good as your skin underneath. Take good care of your skin.

❀ Sunscreen is a must—it is the best thing you can do to keep your skin beautiful year-round! Avoid tanning. Instead, choose a good sunless tanning lotion to get that sun-kissed look.

- ❀ If you have a hard time deciding whether something is right or wrong, ask yourself, "Who will be celebrating if I do this, Jesus or Satan?"

- ❀ Always keep your appointments—even if a better offer comes along.

- ❀ Don't brag about yourself. Your good qualities sound twice as nice coming from others' lips.

- ❀ A smile is more enhancing and attractive than the most expensive makeup.

- ❀ Never, never, never waste time waiting for the phone to ring. Use that time (or any other lonely times) to pamper yourself with a manicure, a favorite book, or writing in your journal. Or think of others who may be lonely and brighten their day by calling them or praying for them.

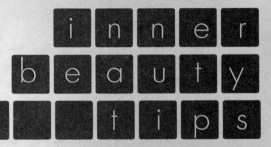

inner beauty tips

point of grace

girls of grace

devotional and Bible study workbook

Make It Real

words, worth, relationships, and me

Contents

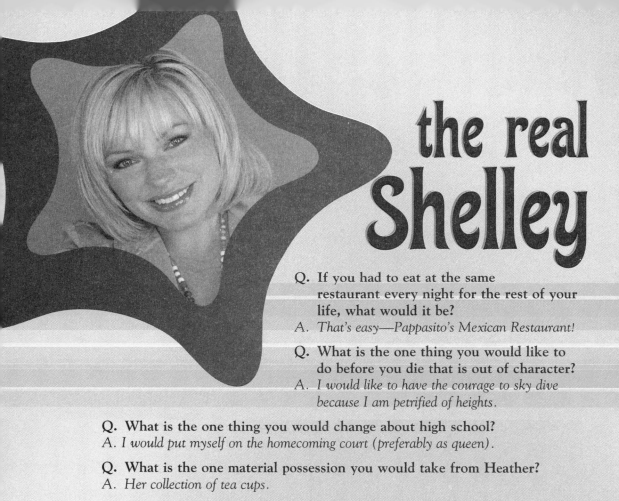

the real Shelley

Q. If you had to eat at the same restaurant every night for the rest of your life, what would it be?
A. *That's easy—Pappasito's Mexican Restaurant!*

Q. What is the one thing you would like to do before you die that is out of character?
A. *I would like to have the courage to sky dive because I am petrified of heights.*

Q. What is the one thing you would change about high school?
A. *I would put myself on the homecoming court (preferably as queen).*

Q. What is the one material possession you would take from Heather?
A. *Her collection of tea cups.*

Q. What characteristic do you love most about yourself?
A. *I have pretty good organizational skills.*

Q. What is the most embarrassing thing about yourself?
A. *I have to wear a girdle almost every day to hold my stomach in . . . I affectionately call it the "torture suit."*

Q. What is the one thing you tried out for and never made?
A. *I tried out for the singing group Truth (several times) and never made it.*

the gift of gab

If we can control our tongues, we'll have the discipline to control ourselves in every other way.

The LORD . . . delights in pure words.
Proverbs 15:26 NLT

Mighty Mouth

We've all done it, haven't we?

You know how it works: our mind formulates some negative or rude comment that makes its way to our tongue faster than a speeding bullet, and *bam!*—out it comes, wounding whoever is in its path. The book of Proverbs says, "Reckless words pierce like a sword" (12:18). Now, I've never actually been pierced by a sword, but something tells me it would really hurt!

Have you ever been really hurt? I don't mean physically, like by a sword or from a broken arm; I mean emotionally raked over the coals. Have the words of someone ever cut to the quick of your soul and made your feelings cry out, "Ouch!"? Let me pose another question to you: Have you ever really hurt someone else? Have you said something that wounded another person deeply, something you wished so badly you could take back, but the bullet had already been fired?

The Gift of Gab—Shelley

If I were to respond to these questions honestly, the answer would be absolutely yes to both. I've dished it out, and I've taken it. Unfortunately, I've done a little more dishing than taking, and I'm just guessing, but something tells me that many of you have, too.

For some reason we females are abundantly blessed with the gift of gab. And we don't always use that gift for good. Now, not all girls are big talkers. I know some beautiful girls who are shy, meek, and absolutely precious—but that is not how I would describe myself. (Well, maybe the "precious" part!)

Seriously though, most girls were just plain born to talk. We're born to yak—about everything! All the time! Without ceasing! I remember in junior high school I thought the verse "Pray without ceasing" said "Talk without ceasing," 'cause that's what I did—all the time. I kid you not.

I would get my grades every quarter, and I would get straight As, almost always. But the conduct grades were another story. There were basically three behavior levels: U was for "unsatisfactory behavior." That was for the boys who did awful stuff like skip class, curse at the teacher—you know the ones. Then there was N for "needs improvement." And of course S stood for "satisfactory," which was achieved by all the kids who didn't suffer from loose lips like I did. Even though

I was pretty book smart, I got straight Ns all the time. My parents would get so mad. Straight As and straight Ns. If I was so smart, how come I needed improvement? I was somewhat of a perfectionist, so I really wanted As and Ss, but if I'd ever gotten any Ss, they would have stood for "shut up"!

Oh well, I suppose all of us girls need a little improvement when it comes to using our mouths the way God intended.

Words That Hurt, Words That Heal

One of the guys in our band used to say, "Words that hurt, words that heal" to remind us to watch our mouths whenever the conversation turned gossipy. Our words have mighty power—for good or for bad. And we can't use the excuse that we just "can't help" what we say. For through the power of the Holy Spirit living in us, we really do have the ability to choose how we use our words. As girls striving to become more Christlike, we can actually choose to use our words to help and heal others, instead of to hurt them. Just because we're girls and come by our talking honestly doesn't mean we have free rein to say what we feel.

Our tongues can turn us into hypocrites before we know it: "If you claim to be religious but don't control your tongue, you are just fooling yourself, and your religion is worthless" (James 1:26 NLT). These are pretty strong words. James is telling us that even if we are religious in other areas of our lives, if we can't control what we say, our religion is *worthless*. That's an awful lot of emphasis on our speech. But if we can control our tongues, we'll have the discipline to control ourselves in every other way. According to James, the tongue is harder to control, or tame, than any wild creature in the world (3:7–8). He doesn't say this to discourage us from trying to control our tongues but to remind us to be very serious in our watch over our mighty mouths.

The book of Proverbs speaks strongly about our tongues, too. It says we are "wicked" when we speak corrupt words: "The godly speak words that are helpful, but the wicked speak only what is corrupt" (Proverbs 10:32 NLT). That seems pretty harsh, but when we consider what is going on in our society today, especially among teenage girls, the description actually is very fitting.

Mean Girls

Some of you, no doubt, have seen the movie *Mean Girls*, starring Lindsay Lohan. Now I'm not supporting the values displayed in this particular flick; but the movie was very enlightening, because it exposes all the ugly things that really happen in our high schools today. It used to be that the word *bully* was associated only with boys, but now bullying is rampant among teenage girls. That is, pushing people around, whether physically or otherwise, just to make yourself feel like a bigger person. Bullying is downright *mean*!

In the movie Cady (pronounced "Katie"), played by Lohan, is the new girl at school. Having been homeschooled her whole life, Cady desperately wants to be accepted at her new high school. She quickly becomes friends with Regina George, the beauty queen who is the self-proclaimed leader of the most popular clique in school, "The Plastics" (who are very aptly named, I might add). Cady is quickly pulled into their backstabbing, cheating, lying ways, even though her conscience tells her that she needs to stay away and that these girls are total fakes and nothing but trouble.

As Cady moves up the social ladder and eventually replaces Regina as the "it" girl, she realizes that she is miserable; she hates herself for the things she has done and for what she has become. She is now just like them.

The Plastics actually have a book called *The Burn Book*, which is full of pictures and hurtful lies and gossip about their classmates. When the book becomes public, it turns the school upside down, wounding everyone. In the end The Plastics are the most miserable of all. The popular Plastics become the bullies that everyone hates—all because of their big mouths. The trouble started not with what they *did* to other students but with what they *said*.

In Ephesians 4:29 the Word of God says, "Don't use foul or abusive language. Let everything you say be good and helpful, so that your words will be an encouragement to those who hear them" (NLT). How's that for a challenge? Talk about weighing every single thing you say. Notice that this verse doesn't say, "Let *most* things you say be good and helpful"; it says, "Let *everything* you say be good and helpful." I know that, for me, this seems almost impossible. But we all know that in Christ all things are possible.

Tips for Taming the Mighty Tongue

We'll talk in the following chapter about getting to the heart of the matter when it comes to controlling our tongues, but for now I'd like to offer you a few practical tips for keeping your tongue tamed.

The Gift of Gab—Shelley

When Gossip Starts, Zip It Up!

There is nothing more powerful than a little silence. If your friends insist on bringing up some juicy stuff, just sit there and don't say a word. If they ask you what's up, tell them you're practicing Tongue Control 101, based on Proverbs 17:27–28: "A truly wise person uses few words; a person with understanding is even-tempered. Even fools are thought to be wise when they keep silent; when they keep their mouths shut, they seem intelligent" (NLT). Now, I'm not saying you're a fool, but we could all glean something from this verse. Trust me, I've had someone use this tip on me before, and the silent treatment is very convincing to the gossiper!

Pretend It's Opposite Day

Whenever you feel a little bullet about to escape your mouth, force yourself to turn it into a positive comment. For example, maybe you're about to say to someone, "I really don't appreciate you liking the same guy I like. I claimed him first!" Instead, how about saying, "The shirt you are wearing is really cute. Where did you get it?" Strive to find a positive and helpful comment, even if it's against your nature at first. Some people might call this tip being fake; I say it's practicing self-control, which is one of the fruits of the Spirit, mind you!

Pray for Your Enemies

This is one of those things that really stinks when you first start doing it. I mean, let's be honest. Who wants to pray for someone who makes your life miserable? But let me tell you, there is something to it. Not only does praying for your enemies soften your heart, but in time, your kindness can affect the other person, too. Prayer is your own secret weapon, and it's available to all girls of grace, thank goodness. It's also very handy, since there is no assembly required!

Consider Yourself

What I mean is, consider how what you are about to say would make you feel if it were spoken to you. If it would be helpful to you, then fire away. If not, it's probably better left inside your mouth.

It's a Daily Process

I know this all sounds wildly impossible to actually live up to, but the fact is, taming the mighty tongue is a daily process that takes time and attention. I promise, though, it will be worth the effort. Slow down and think about your own speeding bullets. Remember this verse from Psalm 34:12–14: "Do any of you want to live a life that is long and good? Then watch your tongue! Keep your lips from telling lies! Turn away from evil and do good. Work hard at living in peace with others" (NLT).

I know I want a life that is long and good. Don't you? Sounds like we now know the secret, so let's get to taming!

STUDY GUIDE

Do My Words Hurt or Heal?

📖 **Opening Scripture:** Read James 1:26. Ask God to speak to you today as you study His Word.

⭐ **Think before You Speak:** If you're like most girls, your words just come out. You freely express your thoughts and feelings. Your sister stains the shirt she borrowed from you, and you give her a piece of your mind. Your brother gets on your nerves, and you respond in a less-than-kind way. It's so much easier to just let our mouths run and run—rather than weighing our words before we speak.

What's your experience? When we are stressed or irritated, we are less likely to think before we speak. What are your words like when you are stressed? _____

_____

_____

What does the Word say? Now look back at James 1:26. What does the verse teach about someone who doesn't "keep a tight rein on his tongue"? _____

_____

_____

Think about it: Worthless! That is a very strong word. It's so easy to think that sinning with our mouths is no big deal. But God says that when our words don't honor Him, we are fooling ourselves and our "religion is worthless." Do you seriously desire for your words to please Him?

❏ Sometimes.

❏ No, I don't want to change.

❏ Yes, my prayer is that God will help me tame my tongue.

❏ _____

Why do you think God puts such a high priority on what we say?

_____

_____

☆ Words Are a Window to the Heart

What does the Word say? Read Matthew 12:34. What does this passage teach about where our words come from? _____

_____

_____

Think about it: Have you ever said something mean and then later wondered where it came from? Matthew 12:34 teaches that hateful words reveal what's inside our hearts. While we often focus on outside appearances and actions, God cares the most about what's inside. He desires for our hearts to be filled with love for others. When you find that your words are mean, take some time to examine your heart. You may need to let God do open-heart surgery on you.

What's your experience? Based on the words you speak, what kind of grade do you think God would give your heart?

- ❏ U: Unsatisfactory behavior
- ❏ N: Needs improvement
- ❏ S: Satisfactory
- ❏ _____

Chances are that you don't have a Burn Book like the one shown in the movie *Mean Girls*, but can you imagine if every hurtful word or lie you had ever spoken was written in a book? Would your book be small like a pamphlet or huge with several volumes? _____

_____

Think about it: A Burn Book can be destroyed, but the effects of hurtful words can last a lifetime. You may remember the childhood saying "Sticks and stones can break my bones, but words will never hurt me." While this is a cute rhyme, it's not necessarily true. A physical bruise or cut may heal, but the pain brought from careless words can last forever.

☆ Things to Guard Against

1. Gossip

What's your experience? Has there ever been a time when you have been hurt by gossip? Describe the situation. How did you feel? _____

_____

_____

Do My Words Hurt or Heal?

Describe a time when you took part in gossip. What were the results?

_____

_____

_____

What does the Word say? Maybe as far as you could see, no one got hurt. It's easy to trick ourselves into thinking that a little gossip is okay. But it's not! Gossip can have devastating consequences. It is a sin against God and against those He has called us to love. Read Proverbs 17:9. What does this verse say happens as a result of gossip?_____

_____

_____

2. Loose Lips

What's your experience? Have you ever struggled with loose lips? Maybe you've said something without thinking, and the damage has been done. If so, describe what happened: _____

_____

_____

Think about it: Have you ever said, "I take that back" after saying something mean? Well, it's important to remember that you can't take something back once you've said it. We can ask for forgiveness, but we can never rewrite history. The results of our words, either good or bad, start the moment we speak them.

What's your experience? Can you remember a time when someone hurt you with his or her words? Even though it may have happened years ago, you can probably remember where you were and the person's tone of voice. Describe the situation and how you felt. _____

_____

_____

_____

3. Lies

What's your experience? Have you ever told a "little white lie" to escape some trouble or make yourself look better?

- ❑ Never. (If so, are you lying now?)
- ❑ Yes, I really struggle with this.
- ❑ Yes, but it's no big deal.
- ❑ Yes, and I want to stop.

What does the Word say? Now read Proverbs 6:16–17. How does God feel about lying? _____

_____

_____

Think about it: God puts lying in the same category as "hands that shed innocent blood." In our human minds, murder seems so much worse than lying. But God doesn't weigh sin the same way we do. All sin is serious to Him, and it should be that way to us, too.

Do My Words Hurt or Heal?

⭐ **Change Is a Daily Process:** Taming the tongue is a lifelong battle. It's not going to happen in a day, a week, or even a year. Just like taming a wild animal, controlling our tongues happens gradually over time. The more you consciously choose to cooperate with God in the area of tongue control, the more you will see positive results. You'll recognize times when you hold your tongue instead of speaking your mind. You'll tell the truth and resist lying. As God changes your heart, your words will change, too. Let's look at some practical ways to surrender our tongues to God's control.

1. Pray. The first step to changing the hurtful words we say is prayer. Before you speak to anyone else each day, ask God to help you rely on Him for strength in controlling your tongue. Ask Him to help you use your words to build others up instead of tearing them down. Pray that He will change your heart so that what comes out of your mouth reflects His love and character. And when you do mess up, confess your sin and then move on.

2. Memorize the Word. As we have seen, when our minds change, so do our words. That's why it's so important to mentally "chew on" the Word of God. Write out some verses that deal with the mighty mouth and keep them handy. Memorize them when you're taking a shower or exercising.

Fill in the blanks: *Read Psalm 34:12–13, and fill in the missing words.

*Use the New International Version for the "Fill in the blanks" sections.

"Whoever of you _____ _____ and desires to see many _____ days, _____ your _____ from _____ and your lips from _____ _____."

3. Ask for help. I don't mean join the support group Bigmouths Anonymous, but you will find that taming the tongue is easier if you don't go it alone. Share with a Christian friend or youth leader your desire to change. Ask her to pray with you and hold you accountable. You may even want to set up a "no-gossip" rule with your friends. When the conversation heads toward gossip, you may want to say a code word you've agreed on with your friends that reminds you to change the subject.

✝ **Living the Word:** Read Proverbs 10:19–21.

• According to this passage, what happens when there are many words? _____

_____

• What practical steps are you going to take so that you learn how to hold your tongue? _____

_____

• Reread verse 21. How can the "lips of the righteous nourish many"?

_____

_____

_____

Do My Words Hurt or Heal?

• Recall a situation where someone else's words "nourished" you. What did that person say, and how did his or her words affect you?

_____

_____

_____

_____

• Describe a time when God used your words to nourish someone else. _____

_____

_____

_____

_____

• Write out a prayer asking God to help you use your words to help others as opposed to hurt them. He is willing to help you change.

_____

_____

_____

_____

_____

_____

_____

_____

Mouth management doesn't start with the mouth at all; it starts with the heart.

The godly think before speaking;
the wicked spout evil words.
Proverbs 15:28 NLT

Mouth Management

Mouth management. Hmm. Interesting term, but what exactly does it mean? We talked in the previous chapter about the negative effects of a loose tongue and saw that most of us girls have a tendency to "gab to jab"! But how do we change what we've been doing for so long? How do we learn to manage our mouths?

The interesting thing is, mouth management doesn't start with the mouth at all. It starts with the heart. Jesus said in Luke 6:45, "For out of the overflow of his heart his mouth speaks." This means that whatever is in your heart just kind of bubbles up and comes out of your mouth! This can be good—or bad—depending on what's in your heart.

Fortunately, God did not leave us alone in the task of guarding our hearts. He's made controlling our hearts and tongues a team effort. So who exactly makes up this team? You, Jesus, and the Holy Spirit. Only with their help do we have the power to override the temptation for jab gabbing!

The Dream Team

It's amazing that two members of the Godhead (Jesus and the Holy Spirit) actually live inside of us. Talk about *dream team*! But does Jesus *really* live in your heart? The Bible says He does: "Christ lives in you, and this is assurance that you will share in his glory" (Colossians 1:27 NLT). But let's back up a minute. Before Christ can live in us, the Bible says we must believe in Jesus as the Son of God and receive Him. If you have never confessed to God that you desire Jesus to be Lord of your life, you can turn to pages 372–73 to find out how.

The first and most important step to mouth management is getting Jesus into your heart. And when Jesus lives in your heart as a "landlord," your heart will be well managed, and you'll stand a lot better chance of using your words wisely—to heal and not to hurt!

The second member of your team is the Holy Spirit. 1 Corinthians 6:19 says, "Your body is the temple of the Holy Spirit, who lives in you and was given to you by God" (NLT). One way to tell whether the Holy Spirit is really living in your heart is to check to see if His fruit is in your life.

When you look at the list of the Spirit's fruit in Galatians 5:22–23, it's amazing how many of them are tied directly to our speech. Have you ever noticed that? Look how some of the fruit of the Spirit can be directly tied to the words we say (or don't say!):

- Love—telling those who are closest to us that we love them
- Joy—speaking cheerfully to encourage those around us
- Peace—helping to resolve conflicts
- Patience—knowing when it's better *not* to speak but rather wait
- Faithfulness—being a loyal friend, with no backstabbing
- Self-control—again, knowing when to hold back

All of these traits are evidence to the rest of the world that God lives in our hearts.

Now that you've met your other team members, you're ready to move to the next step, which is taking an honest look inside your heart and cleaning it up so that what bubbles out is *good*.

A Look Inside

Even with the dream team living inside your heart, you still have to make your own choices about how you manage your mouth. And this means managing your thoughts before you speak. The only way to manage your thoughts is to manage your heart—and this starts with honest self-examination.

Even though examining your heart can be uncomfortable (oh, all right—it is sometimes downright *painful*), you have to assess what's there before you can clean up your thoughts and speech. You need to take an honest look at yourself so you can discover why you do the things you do and say the things you say.

The Gift of Gab—Shelley

I've always loved to kid around and crack jokes, many times at someone else's expense. When I consider my attempts to get laughs, I have to chalk a lot of it up to my personality. I've always been this way—loud, boisterous, joking all the time. Heather says that I say the stuff that other people think but would never say. (I'm not sure that's always a good thing, however.) I just genuinely love making people laugh.

Lately I've come to believe that my desire to make others laugh is really a gift from God—and I know I should use it carefully and wisely. But I never really thought of it as a gift until I read Frank Peretti's book *No More Bullies*.

Author Frank Peretti is best known for his book *This Present Darkness*, but his lesser-known book *No More Bullies* has some of the best material on the subject of bullies that I've ever read. In it he says: "God says that it is right to respect my fellow man, to love him, to care for him, and to protect him. It is wrong to abuse, tease, taunt, intimidate, hurt, harass, or violate anyone. Taking it a step further, to demean another person is sin. When we indulge in such practices, we are doing so in direct disobedience to our Lord Jesus Christ."[1] I love his directness, don't you? I mean, let's call a spade a spade. When we demean anyone, we are a sinner at her worst! This is why it's so important to continually keep our hearts in check—so we won't commit these sins against God. How we relate to others is serious business and needs to be treated as such.

Toward the end of that book, I read something that really changed me, forever, I hope. Peretti tells about a bully he attended junior high school with who was nicknamed Mr. Muscles. Mr. Muscles used his physical strength to push people around. Peretti says that the bully was completely misusing his gift from God, and luckily, Frank got his courage up enough to tell him so. He told him, "*Any* gift you receive from God is not for yourself, but for others. The strong are to protect the weak; those with abundance are blessed so they can help the needy; the smart and the wise are gifted to help the befuddled and foolish."[2]

When I examine my heart and think about my gift of humor, I am totally convinced by this thought. How dare I ever use my gift to hurt others, all for a stupid laugh or to make myself seem funny! My gift of humor is not even *for* me; it's for those around me! Just like Mr. Muscles was there to *protect* the weak, not to bully them. I had never thought of it that way before. The fact that we even *can* talk should be considered a gift—a gift to be used for the gain of others, not of ourselves.

More Heart Examination

Most people probably wouldn't know this about me, but if I were to be honest, I'd have to say that I deal with jealousy in my heart. If I were to really get to the bottom of things, the reason I may not use my mouth to compliment someone when I should is because of my own jealous pride. It's the weirdest thing, but I have trouble paying people compliments and building them up. I have no idea why. The only thing I can figure is that I'm dealing with some kind of deep-seated envy in my heart. Now that I think about it, I'm sure of it.

For example, I may look at a friend's new haircut, think it looks totally awesome, but then not say how good it looks. Isn't that ridiculous? Do I wish somewhere deep inside that *my* hair would look that great? Or maybe I just wish *she* didn't look so great. I really think that's it. How ugly is that!? How prideful of my heart! Seems to me that Shelley is taking up a little more room than Jesus and the Holy Spirit in my heart and that I need to move on over.

Lately I've really been working on saying the good things I think—and not just the negative things. For whatever reason, it's so much easier to speak the negative and to keep the positive inside. It should be the complete opposite, but there's that sin we have to deal with. I hate that! I mean, just to admit this about myself isn't easy, but at least it's the first step.

What's in Your Heart?

Is there something in your own heart that needs to be examined? Something that's bubbling up from your heart and coming out your mouth that is less than nice? I guess words really do show the real you. The Bible says it so clearly: "A good person produces good deeds from a good heart, and an evil person produces evil deeds from an evil heart. Whatever is in your heart determines what you say" (Luke 6:45 NLT). "For as he thinks in his heart, so *is* he" (Proverbs 23:7 NKJV).

Your heart is what God will look at in the end. I read a very sobering verse in Matthew that you may have never considered. I don't know about you, but it will make me inventory my heart before I use loose talk again: "You must give an account on judgment day of every idle word you speak. The words you say now reflect your fate then; either you will be justified by them or you will be condemned" (12:36–37 NLT). This verse is the ultimate reason for becoming a good "mouth manager."

It all begins, and ends, with our hearts.

Lord, Change My Heart

📖 **Opening Scripture:** Ask God to speak to you in a specific way as you study His Word. Then read Luke 6:45.

⭐ **Take a Look Inside:** Have you ever hung up the phone or finished a conversation with someone and realized that you had just said a "zinger"? A zinger is one of those ugly things we say to or about someone that we should have just left unspoken. Zingers can slip out of our mouths before we even know what hit us. Where do they come from?

Fill in the blanks: Reread Luke 6:45 and fill in the missing words.

"The _____ man brings good things out of the _____ stored up in his _____, and the _____ man brings _____ things out of the evil _____ up in his _____. For out of the overflow of his _____ his _____ speaks."

What does it mean? According to this verse, where do our words come from? _____

_____

Think about it: When evil or unkind things come out of our mouths, what does that tell us about the condition of our hearts? _____

_____

_____

What's your experience? Has there ever been a time when you said something and then realized that the mean thing you said reflected what was going on inside of you? If so, describe the situation. _____

_____

_____

_____

☆ Praise or Poison?

What does it mean? Read James 3:7–10. What do you think verse 8 means when it says the tongue is "full of deadly poison"? _____

_____

_____

_____

What two opposite things can come from the tongue?

- ❏ Happy and sad songs
- ❏ Screaming and whispering
- ❏ Praise and cursing
- ❏ Crudity and sophistication
- ❏ Rudeness and politeness

Think about it: Our tongues have the capacity for good and for evil. When we use our tongues to hurt others, it shows that our hearts need change. If you struggle with your words, you might need to take a long, hard look at what is going on inside. Maybe you have jealousy, like Shelley described, or bitterness or hate inside. Ask God to reveal what changes you need to let Him make in your heart so that your words will bless those around you.

The Gift of Gab—Study Guide

☆ **We Are Responsible:** Have you ever noticed that in our society, no one wants to take personal responsibility for things they do wrong? We try to avoid consequences, and we certainly don't want punishment. It's the same way for the things people say. They want to say whatever they feel without suffering any cost. Well, God's Word says that life doesn't work that way. One day everyone who has ever lived will be held accountable for every word he or she has spoken. That's a sobering thought, isn't it?

What does the Word say? Read Matthew 12:36–37. According to this verse, for what will we be held accountable on the day of judgment?

- ❏ What we wore
- ❏ What we said
- ❏ Who we dated
- ❏ How much we prayed

Think about it: I don't know about you, but that verse really makes me think about some of the dumb things I've said. I wish I could erase some whole conversations I have had and some of the careless ways I have spoken to and about someone else.

What is your reaction to Matthew 12:36–37? _____

_____

_____

Lord, Change My Heart

What do you think? Does knowing that you will have to give account for every word make you want to change the way you talk to and about others? Why or why not? _____

_____

_____

Think about it: Maybe the thought of being responsible for every word makes you feel overwhelmed. You can remember all of the horrible things you've said, and it makes you want to give up hope of changing. You think you might as well move to a remote tropical island where you'll never speak to anyone again. Well, don't be discouraged. God will help you tame your tongue as you rely on Him and His power. You can move forward, knowing that He is quick to forgive and to help you change.

☆ **Filter Your Words:** Have you ever used a filter to separate two things? Maybe you were dividing liquid from something else or taking out something impure from the pure. In the same way, maybe you need to let God put a filter on your mouth. If so, the following verse is a great filter that will help you know what to say and what to leave unspoken. If our words don't fit the description in the verse, we should consider just keeping our mouths shut!

Fill in the blanks: Read Ephesians 4:29 and fill in the missing words.

The Gift of Gab—Study Guide

"Do not let any _____ talk come out of your _____, but only what is _____ for building _____ up according to their _____, that it may _____ those who _____."

What do you think? How can our words build others up? _____
_____
_____

What's your experience? Has someone ever said something to you that built you up according to what you needed? If so, describe what that person said and how his or her words made you feel. _____
_____
_____

Pray about it: Spend a few moments asking God to help you speak only words that will benefit those who listen to them. You may even want to add this prayer to your daily list. Pray this before you get out of bed in the morning and before you speak to anyone other than God.

✔ **Try This:** Use the space below to make a list of some positive ways you have used your words this week. Maybe you've helped a friend with a problem or a younger sibling with homework. Or you may have encouraged someone who was having a hard day. You might have told a friend about the love of Jesus and how to know Him better. These are some of the great ways we can use the gift of gab. Look over your list, and ask God to help you take advantage of more situations like these. _____

_____

_____

_____

What's your experience? After you finish that list, make a list of some of the negative ways you've used your words. Maybe you talked back to a parent or teacher or snapped at your little brother. You may have passed along a zinger to an unsuspecting friend. Or you may have spoken words of revenge when someone hurt you. _____

_____

_____

_____

Pray about it: Prayerfully read through this list, asking God to show if there is anyone He wants you to apologize to. If there is someone, or several people, call them today when you finish this lesson, and tell them you're sorry. Ask God to forgive you, and then pray that He will help you choose to hold your tongue the next time you're tempted to say something ugly. Remember, He is ready to forgive you and help you change from the inside out.

✝ **Living the Word:** Read Psalm 141:3.

The Gift of Gab—Study Guide

• Rewrite this verse in your own words. _____

_____

_____

• What practical steps can you take this week to guard your words?

_____

_____

• Are there situations where you are more vulnerable to sinning with your mouth? If so, list those below. Then beside each one, write a way that you will be on guard against sinning with your words when you're in that situation. _____

_____

_____

_____

_____

• Now write Psalm 141:3 on a note card, and put it in your backpack or purse. Whenever you reach for your lip gloss or lipstick, read that verse. This will help you remember that your mouth can be used for good and evil. Choose to let God use it for good.

Did you know

that our hearts

actually teach our lips

what to say?

He who guards his mouth preserves his life,
But he who opens wide his lips shall have destruction.
Proverbs 13:3 NKJV

Sanctified Gossip

With all this talk about how we're *not* supposed to talk, you may be wondering why God even gave you a mouth! It may seem the freedom of speech is more trouble than it's worth.

So what are we to do with these out-of-control contraptions, anyway? Is there anything we actually *can* say? Fortunately for us, girls, there is! I was privileged just a couple of months ago to hear Beth Moore speak at a Bible study in Houston, Texas. And she used a term in one of her illustrations that really got my attention. She talked about "sanctified gossip." When I heard that, I thought to myself, *Hmm, sounds like something I need to check into.*

Beth was speaking, as she often does, about the power of women in the Bible. In Mark 16 three women—Mary Magdalene, Mary the mother of James, and Salome—came to visit the tomb where Jesus had been put after His death on the cross. I'm sure you know the story. When the women arrived, they found that the large stone, which had covered the opening to the tomb, had been moved away; and Jesus was nowhere to be found. Instead, an angel greeted them: "You seek Jesus of Nazareth, who was crucified. He is risen! He is not here" (Mark 16:6 NKJV). Then he said, "But go and tell His disciples— and Peter—that He is going before you into Galilee" (v. 7 NKJV).

Did you get that? The angel commanded the women to *go* and *tell*. The stuff that girls love to do naturally! And besides that, the very first people who heard the greatest news that ever was or ever will be received by humankind— that Jesus Christ had risen from the dead—were three women. Not three men. Three women. Then just a couple of verses down, Jesus Himself first appeared after his triumph over death to Mary Magdalene, a woman who began to spread what Beth Moore so suitably calls "the first ever recorded case of sanctified gossip"!

My friends, it was not an accident that Jesus chose women first to get the Word out. He knew we could do it! I believe it was completely by design. Telling the good news of Christ is by far the very best thing we can be spreading around. In fact, we are commanded to use our mouths to tell others about the awesome and noncondemning love of God.

Sanctified Gossip

People in this day and age really need to hear this news! The world we live in is so depressing sometimes that we can't even think straight. Using our mouths to witness and show God's love to others would be using them exactly the way they were made to be used.

Since most of us girls love to gossip so much, then let's do just that! But let's *sanctify* our gossip! Is that even possible? I think it is! Let's break it down. The word *gossip* means idle talk or rumor, especially about the person or private affairs of others. So obviously, this act in and of itself is a no-no. But *sanctified* means made holy, to purify or free from sin. So if we can take our "idle talk" about others and purify it—free it from sinful language—then all of a sudden, whatever we're saying will most likely bring glory to God instead of defame Him (and the person the comment is about). Sanctifying our words, along with our general "mouth management" as we discussed in the last chapter, begins in our minds and hearts.

Unsanctified Garbage

Did you know our hearts actually teach our lips what to say? "The heart of the wise teaches his mouth, and adds learning to his lips. Pleasant words are like a honeycomb, sweetness to the soul and health to the bones" (Proverbs 16:23–24 NKJV). This reminds us again that, sooner or later, whatever is in our hearts will inevitably bubble up out of our mouths. So it's our job to control the stuff that gets inside us. Just as eating junk food 24/7 will make us miserable, feeding our minds garbage will do the same. Chronic overeating of foods that are bad for you will make you gain weight and become unhealthy.

The Gift of Gab—Shelley

Likewise, chronically watching R-rated movies, reading sex-centered fashion magazines, and listening to music with raunchy lyrics will make you spiritually unhealthy.

Don't worry, I'm not going to preach to you or try to assume the role of your mom, but I am asking you to listen up for just a minute. *You cannot keep these kinds of habits, not even one of them, and be unaffected by them.* In some way, I promise, they will bring you down. I'm so tired of hearing girls say, "Oh, but I just like the groove; I'm not even listening to the lyrics." That is impossible, no matter how strong you are. Girls, we must run from every unholy thing we possibly can, because the fact remains, if we put the garbage in, it's gonna come out—either in our actions or in our words.

I wish we could have some sort of selective hearing or sight loss as Christians living in our world today. But we can't. What we read and watch and listen to affects us. Let's face it: we all like to read some of those magazines or watch shows like *The O.C.* I do, too. But we can't sanctify the episodes or the movies before we feed them to our minds, so we're better off not even tempting ourselves. It's a struggle for me every single day. Should I watch? Should I not? Should I listen? Should I not?

If you can make the decision to make better choices about what you allow to go into your heart and mind, you will discover some amazing results. As you spend more time with God and less time with the world, your speech will begin to "sanctify" itself. You will have the power to compliment others, tell the truth, respect your parents, be gracious and thankful—the rewards are just endless. Proverbs 15:4 says, "A wholesome tongue is a tree of life, but perverseness in it breaks the spirit" (NKJV). I want my tongue to be a "tree of life," don't you?

Every Day Is a New Day

I love being a Christian for so many reasons, but I think one of the best things about it is the ability to have a fresh start every day. As Christians, if we confess our sins, God is faithful and will forgive us and make us clean again (see 1 John 1:9). In this and the previous two chapters, some of you have probably been convinced you've been using your tongue. We've talked a lot about gossiping, bullying, and backbiting; and we all probably agree that it's wrong. But now it's time for us girls to come together and put a stop to it.

It's time to start spreading "sanctified gossip" and lifting up our brothers and sisters. It's time to focus on the positive impact our words can make today. Even though we may not see the difference now, our words can affect lives for years to come. We have the girl power and the big mouths to do it!

Making a Fresh Start

Perhaps my favorite thing about the book I mentioned in the previous chapter, *No More Bullies*, is at the end of the book when Peretti gives us advice about making a fresh start:

> All it takes is a decision, a pivotal moment when you decide you will put a stop to the bullying and abuse and begin treating everyone who passes your way as a priceless, precious, miraculous creation of God, a person for whom Jesus Christ bled and died, a person who matters to God just as much as you do.
>
> The first step is to wake up to what you've done and what you may still be doing. Admit your sins honestly before God, ask him for forgiveness, and then declare that from this day forward, with God's help, your bullying and malicious teasing days are over. You will begin to treat every person as valuable, even sacred.[1]

Phew! Do you think we can do it? I challenge you to make a commitment to yourself and to God, along with whomever may have done this Bible study with you, that from this day forward, the words that flow from your mouth will be words of love and life.

Pray for me, and I'll pray for you, for this will not be an easy task. Remember that we have the power to speak life or death to someone's soul; it should be an easy choice. Happy gabbing!

STUDY GUIDE

Words of Life

📖 **Opening Scripture:** Begin by reading John 3:16. This may be a familiar verse to you, so ask God to give you a heart to hear from Him in a new way today.

☆ **The Very Best News of All:** Have you ever received really great news? Maybe you made the team or received a call from Mr. Wonderful. You just had to tell your best friend what happened, and you couldn't wait. You tracked her down and shouted into the phone, "Guess what?" When good things happen to us, we just have to tell others—God made us that way.

Fill in the blanks: Reread John 3:16 and fill in the missing words.

"For _____ so _____ the world that he _____ his _____ and only _____, that _____ believes in Him shall not _____ but have _____ life."

I can't think of any better news than this verse. We were separated from God because of the sin we chose, and God made a way for us to escape eternal death and punishment.

What does it mean? How did He make the way for us to have eternal life?

_____

_____

_____

Think about it: Has there ever been a time when you shared God's free gift of eternal life? If so, describe when and what happened. If not, what words would you use to share this gift? (Turn to pages 372–73 for an example.) _____

_____

_____

_____

What's your experience? Who was the first person to share the good news about Jesus with you? How did this person do it, and what did he or she say? _____

_____

_____

_____

☆ **God's Heart for People:** Many of us have heard the story about Jesus' death on the cross so many times that we've become callous to it. We just take it for granted that the God of the whole universe became a man so He could suffer and pay the price for our sins. Maybe you saw Mel Gibson's movie *The Passion of the Christ*. If so, were you struck by the enormous suffering and pain that Jesus experienced on your behalf? It was unbelievable. Even though the movie was probably the most accurate representation of the crucifixion that most of us will ever see, the real event was far worse than any movie could depict. God loves people so much that He was willing to go to extreme measures to save us.

What does the Word say? Read 2 Peter 3:9. According to this verse, what is God's wish for all people?

- ❏ For them to read the Bible
- ❏ For them to stop littering
- ❏ For none of them to perish
- ❏ For them to learn about Jesus

What do you think? What does 2 Peter 3:9 show us about God's heart?

_____

_____

_____

Pray about it: Spend a few minutes asking God to give you a burden for those who don't know Him. Ask Him to let you see people like He does and to give you the boldness to share with them so they can have a personal relationship with Him.

⭐ **Sharing His Love:** Imagine that your friend found the cure for cancer. Maybe she was experimenting in chemistry class and somehow stumbled upon a rare formula that would heal everyone in the world suffering from the disease. You immediately realized that this was such great news that you needed to get the word out. You started to run off to call a national news station, but your friend stopped you. She whispered to you that she wasn't going to tell anyone and didn't want you to, either. She had decided to keep the cure to herself. What would you think?

Words of Life

Obviously, you would be shocked to realize that she wasn't going to share this great news. Her selfish decision would cost many people their lives. It would be a great tragedy that the cure had been found, but the person who found it wouldn't share it.

Think about it: Isn't this the way it is with us and our salvation in Jesus? If we're Christians, we know the "cure" for sin and the way to have a saving relationship with God. Not sharing the message of eternal salvation through Jesus Christ is a far greater tragedy than not sharing the cure for cancer.

What does the Word say? Read Matthew 28:19–20. What are we, as Christians, commanded to do? _____

_____

_____

_____

⭐ **Called to Be a Witness:** Have you ever watched a TV show that had a courtroom scene? If you have, you know that when a witness is called to the bench, he or she swears to tell "the truth, the whole truth, and nothing but the truth." The Bible calls on Christians to be witnesses to the truth as well.

What does the Word say? Read John 14:6. According to this verse, how does Jesus describe Himself? _____

_____

_____

_____

_____

What do you think? What is the only way to have a relationship with God?

- ❑ Going to church
- ❑ Being born in a Christian family
- ❑ Having a relationship with Jesus Christ
- ❑ Being a good person

Think about it: Since Jesus is the truth, when we're called to share the truth as witnesses, that means we're sharing about Him. You don't have to know a bunch of Bible verses or fancy terms to be a witness. Witnesses simply tell others what has happened in their lives.

What's your experience? If you were to share with an unbeliever what God has done in your life, what would you say? Take some time to write about your life before you became a Christian, when you did become a Christian, and what your life has been like since. _____

_____

_____

_____

_____

_____

_____

Words of Life

✔ **Try This:** Take some time to find some Bible verses that tell about the love of Jesus. Two to include are John 3:16 and John 14:6 from this lesson. Now write these verses on a front or back page in your Bible so that when you have a chance to share with someone about God's love, you'll easily find them. You may also want to copy them on a note card to slip in your backpack or purse.

✝ **Living the Word:** Read Matthew 5:14–16.

• What do you think verse 14 means by "you are the light of the world"? _____

_____

• In what ways can you let your light shine so that others want to know more about Jesus? _____

_____

_____

• List one person you are going to share Jesus' love with this week. Now write a prayer asking Him to prepare his or her heart to hear— and to prepare your heart to be a witness of the truth. _____

_____

_____

_____

_____

_____

the real Denise

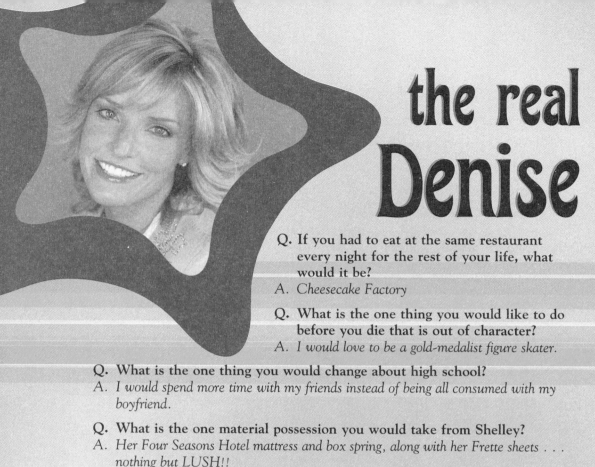

Q. If you had to eat at the same restaurant every night for the rest of your life, what would it be?
A. *Cheesecake Factory*

Q. What is the one thing you would like to do before you die that is out of character?
A. *I would love to be a gold-medalist figure skater.*

Q. What is the one thing you would change about high school?
A. *I would spend more time with my friends instead of being all consumed with my boyfriend.*

Q. What is the one material possession you would take from Shelley?
A. *Her Four Seasons Hotel mattress and box spring, along with her Frette sheets . . . nothing but LUSH!!*

Q. What characteristic do you love most about yourself?
A. *My bubbly personality.*

Q. What is the most embarrassing thing about yourself?
A. *I have ugly feet . . . bunions and all.*

Q. What is the one thing you tried out for and never made?
A. *I tried out for the Opryland Theme Park stage show and got the big fat NO!!*

becoming who you really are

God has created you with your own unique set of gifts and abilities, your own personality, and your own special look.

*I praise you because I am fearfully and
wonderfully made; your works are wonderful,
I know that full well.*

Psalm 139:14

If the Shoe Fits, Wear It

It's amazing how much our closets reveal about who we are. The kinds of clothes we wear are almost like a uniform—you know, like the uniforms doctors, policemen, soldiers, and others wear to show the world who they are. What you wear makes a statement about who you are.

Take a look inside your closet. What kind of clothes do you see? Sporty? Trendy? Preppy? Casual? Do you have cheerleader outfits, basketball clothes, or tights and leotards for dance class? Do you choose comfort over fashion or the other way around? We all have different styles and ways of doing things.

In the same way, each of our hearts has its own closet as well. As we go through this chapter and the next two chapters, I want each of you to open wide the closet doors of your heart and take a good look at yourself. Don't worry. No one else will see. Just you and God, alone. And He loves you just the way you are right now—even if your heart's closet isn't in perfect order. I don't know anyone's that is! In this chapter we'll talk about *discovering* who God designed you to be and then *becoming* that beautiful girl of grace.

Speaking of girls of grace, it amazes me every day how different the four of us in Point of Grace are. Just taking a look at each of our closets will show you some of our differences. For instance, if you were to look in Shelley's or Leigh's closet, you would find them to be very neat, tidy, and organized. Shelley's clothes are organized by seasons, then divided by pants, skirts, shirts, etc. Leigh's would be set up in a similar way but color-coded as well. Now, Heather's or mine would look quite different. *Messy* would be Shelley's choice word for our closets. Mine might look a little more organized than Heather's, but let's just say that organization is not either of our strengths. Even when I do manage to clean out my closet a bit, it is a disaster within a week.

Besides our neatness—or lack thereof—our closets also show our differences by the kinds of clothes you'd find in them. In my closet you'd find a wide variety: golf clothes, singing clothes, take-the-kids-to-the-park clothes, and trendy stuff. Now, Shelley's closet would have a little less variety, and her clothes would be more classic and traditional. I have these crazy high-heeled black, long boots that Shelley would never want to wear. She has some beautiful classic sling-backs that I would probably never find anything to go with.

Just as our closets are different, so are our personalities. I'm hyper, bouncy, competitive, and always want to be on the go. Heather is laid back, a deep thinker, and takes things in stride. It takes a lot to stress her out. Shelley is in control and a great leader. She always knows how to motivate the rest of us. Leigh is the encourager, always wanting to help out where she is needed. She is a very faithful and devoted friend. I love how God chose to make us all unique. "For we are His workmanship, created in Christ Jesus for good works, which God prepared beforehand that we should walk in them" (Ephesians 2:10 NKJV). Each of us was created by God, but we all have our own shoes to walk in.

Discover Your SHAPE

Just like God has made the four of us different in Point of Grace, He has created you with your own unique set of gifts and abilities, your own personality, and your own special look. In fact, the Bible says that God actually shaped you, He formed you to be just whom He wanted you to be: "Your hands shaped me and made me" (Job 10:8). You were shaped by the God of the universe. But how many girls are satisfied with the shape God has given them? Even the most beautiful models say they would like to change something about themselves. Especially in America we are obsessed with our shape. The epidemic of eating disorders proves this.

But the truth is, God has shaped you in a unique way to serve Him. He has special things in mind for you. In the book of Isaiah, God says, "The people I formed for myself that they may proclaim my praise" (43:21). It's pretty hard to broadcast God's praises when we aren't happy with the way He created us. But we can become happy with how He's created us when we understand the beauty of our own unique SHAPE. In Rick Warren's book *The Purpose Driven Life*, he makes the word *shape* into an acronym.

Spiritual gifts

Heart

Abilities

Personality

Experience

You have been given each of the features above—hand-selected by God just for you—to be used for Him. Let's take a minute to look inside the closet of who God created you to be.

Spiritual Gifts

According to Rick Warren, spiritual gifts are special gifts given only to Christians and given for the express purpose of serving God. Here's how the apostle Paul explains it in Ephesians: "Christ gave each one of us the special gift of grace, showing how generous he is. And Christ gave gifts to people—

he made some to be apostles, some to be prophets, some to go and tell the Good News, and some to have the work of caring for and teaching God's people. Christ gave those gifts to prepare God's holy people for the work of serving, to make the body of Christ stronger" (4:7, 11–12 NCV).

God has given you spiritual gifts, too. You may have the gift of making people feel comfortable or the ability to see into people's hearts and sympathize with their hurts. Your gift might be encouragement or generosity or sharing your faith. Maybe you have the gift of organization or leadership. Whatever gift God has given you, you can be sure that He intends that you use it for Him. Sometimes it takes us awhile to figure out what our spiritual gifts are—and that's okay. Ask God to show you where you fit in. Ask some of your friends or teachers where they think you fit in. You'll figure it out with a little time, prayer, and patience.

Heart

When we talk about *heart*, we're talking about what you love to do, what you're passionate about. Think about it for a minute. What do you love to do? What makes your heart beat fast? What are you passionate about? When you answer these questions, you'll know a little more about the person that God created you to be and a little bit more about how you fit into His plan.

Abilities

Pastor Warren says that your *abilities* are "the natural talents you were born with."[1] When you were born, you had in your genes the ability to do certain things well. What are you good at? What comes natural to you? Some people have a hard time coming up with an answer to these questions, but studies have shown that the average person has five hundred to seven hundred different skills and abilities. That's a lot! Even if you only tap into a fraction of yours, what a difference you could make! "Whatever you do, do it all for the glory of God" (1 Corinthians 10:31).

Personality

God has purposely created different kinds of personalities—and all of them are valuable and needed.

I read a book several years ago titled *Personality Plus* by Florence Littauer.[2] I highly recommend that you read it, too. In it Florence explains the four main personality types (popular sanguines, powerful cholerics, peaceful phlegmatics, and perfect melancholies) and helps us recognize and be thankful for our own uniqueness. She even includes a few fun personality tests to help you understand yourself a little better.

The first thing you have to understand is that there are no right or wrong personalities. Our God is a God of variety, and He created different personality types on purpose and for a purpose. "Now there are different kinds of spiritual gifts, but it is the same Holy Spirit who is the source of them all. There are different kinds of service in the church, but it is the same Lord we are serving. There are different ways God works in our lives, but it is the same God who does the work through all of us" (1 Corinthians 12:4–6 NLT). Your particular personality type is a gift from God. It may need some refinement and maturing, but your basic personality is *good*.

Experience

Our life experiences—good and bad—also play a big part in shaping us into who we are. You've had all kinds of experiences: family experiences and educational experiences, job experiences, and spiritual experiences. All of these have helped shape you into the person you are. And you've also had painful experiences. And in a strange way, our painful experiences can end up being a blessing—if we let them.

Just think about it a minute: it's the painful experiences that most prepare us to help someone else, because when we've experienced pain, we better understand the pain of others. Paul put it this way: "Praise be to the God and Father of our Lord Jesus Christ, the Father of compassion and the God of all comfort, who comforts us in all our troubles, so that we can comfort those in any trouble with the comfort we ourselves have received from God" (2 Corinthians 1:3–4). See what he's saying? When you hurt and are comforted by God, then you are able to pass that comfort on to other hurting people.

And besides helping us be more sympathetic to others in pain, if we let it, pain can also help us move closer to God. In addition to that, it gives us a new perspective of what's truly important in life. So you see, our experiences—even the painful ones—are part of what shapes us into who we are.

Be What God Made You to Be

God has given us a SHAPE of His own choosing—He has given us spiritual gifts, heart, abilities, personality, and experiences. This next verse says it all: "Since we find ourselves fashioned into all these excellently formed and marvelously functioning parts in Christ's body, let's just go ahead and be what we were made to be" (Romans 12:5–6 THE MESSAGE). That is a beautiful challenge: *just go ahead and be what God made you to be.*

There's an old Danish proverb that says, "What you are is God's gift to you; what you do with yourself is your gift to God." Dig into your closet today. Pull out those unique qualities God has given you and wear them proudly. It's okay to admire the qualities God has put into the closets of others and the people He has shaped them to be—even to compliment them for it. We all need to be noticed for our own style and personality. But be content with the beautiful girl of grace God has called *you* to be.

So wear whatever "shoe" God has given you. Don't try to cram your foot into a shoe that doesn't fit. Don't be like Cinderella's older sisters, who wanted so badly to be someone they weren't that they tried to stuff their feet into a too-small shoe.

You can choose to develop the talents and skills that go with your personality and become a truly wonderful, well-developed woman; or you can struggle in vain to try to develop talents and skills that belong to someone else. But that shoe will never fit. Oh, you can force it and fake it and try to wear shoes that just don't fit, but your feet will *always* hurt—and you definitely will not live happily ever after.

making it real

STUDY GUIDE

Who He Made Me to Be

📖 **Opening Scripture:** Ask God to speak to you in a specific way as you study His Word today. Then read Psalm 139:13–14.

⭐ **Accepting Who God Made You to Be:** If you could be anyone in the world, who would you be? Would you be a famous actress or a model? Or maybe you would morph into someone who goes to your school. She doesn't seem to have any problems, has the perfect wardrobe, and has never struggled with her weight. Isn't it easy to look at someone else's life and think that she has it made? We do it all the time. When we flip through magazines, we wish we could have the bodies of the models on the pages. Watching our favorite TV shows reminds us of how funny and stylish we don't feel. When we listen to what the world says, it's easy to forget that we are God's unique creations. That's why it's important that we look to His Word to define who we are.

What's your experience? Have you ever longed to be someone else rather than who God made you? If so, who? _____
Even this person would want to change something about herself. The key isn't altering who we are, but accepting and embracing it.

Fill in the blanks: Reread Psalm 139:13–14 and fill in the missing words.

"For you _____ my inmost being; you _____ me together in my _____ womb. I praise you because I am _____

Who He Made Me to Be

and _____ made; your works are _____, I know that full well."

What do you think? How does that verse make you feel about yourself?

- ❏ Excited that God made me special
- ❏ Sad that I have never known this before
- ❏ It doesn't really make a difference in how I feel
- ❏ _____

What's your experience? Have you ever received a handmade present? Maybe someone knitted you a sweater or painted you a picture. Or perhaps someone wrote you a song or poem. If so, how did you feel about the gift? _____

_____

_____

Think about it: Psalm 139 says that God "knit" you. What an amazing thought: the God of the universe has especially designed you! He could have spoken the word and made all people the same. But He didn't. He made you a one-of-a-kind so that He could use you in the unique plan He has for your life.

⭐ **Designed for a Purpose:** Acts 17:26–27 teaches that God even determined where and when we would live. According to these verses, why did God create us?

- ❏ To witness to others
- ❏ To love others

Becoming Who You Really Are—Study Guide

❏ To seek Him

❏ To serve Him

What do you think? God created you so that you would seek Him and know Him. How well are you fulfilling that purpose? _____

_____

When we know God, we learn more about His plans for our lives. We come to realize that God has designed each one of us with a unique SHAPE.

⭐ **What SHAPE Are You?** I'm not talking about whether you are tall and thin or short and round or somewhere in between. According to Rick Warren in *The Purpose Driven Life*, there are five things that go into making the SHAPE of who you are.

1. Spiritual gifts. God gives each Christian at least one spiritual gift so that we can use it to serve Him. It may take you a little while to figure out which ones you have; but the more you serve Him, the more your spiritual gifts will be revealed. Sometimes people take inventories that help them discover what their gifts are. Another way is to ask those who know us best.

What's your experience? Do you have any idea what spiritual gift or gifts you might have? If so, write them here._____

_____

_____

Who He Made Me to Be

What does the Word say? Read Romans 12:4–8. Why is it important that there are all kinds of gifts given to different Christians? _____

_____

_____

Your gifts may not be the most visible gifts, like those of your pastor or youth leader, but they are just as important. Be sure to "open" them and use them.

2. Heart. What gives you the greatest joy? (And I'm not talking about shopping.) Maybe it's taking care of children or serving those less fortunate. You might have a desire to create art that glorifies God.

What do you think? List some of the passions of your heart. _____

_____

_____

Think about it: Are you using these passions to serve Him? If you have a heart for children, then why not volunteer to work in your church children's program? What are some practical ways you can glorify God with the passions in your heart?_____

_____

_____

_____

_____

_____

3. Abilities. You may not think you have them—but you do! Are you a fast runner or an especially loyal friend? Maybe you are good in science or can take really great pictures.

Think about it: List some of your abilities. _____

_____

_____

How can you use these abilities to honor God?_____

_____

_____

4. Personality. Look back at Psalm 139:13–14. Did you know that when God made you, He gave you a particular "bent" or personality? While your parents and environment have also shaped you, a lot of your personality was determined even before you were born. Are you laid back? Energetic? A leader? A thinker?

What do you think? If your best friend had to describe your personality in three words, what would she say? _____

_____

5. Experience. Think back over your personal history from the time you were born until now. God can use all of the things that have happened to you, good and bad, to help others and honor Him. No one else has the exact same experiences you have.

Who He Made Me to Be

Think about it: If you had to title the story of your life, what would it be?

_____

_____

⭐ **God Wants to Use You:** Read 1 Corinthians 2:9. According to this verse, describe the plans that God has for those who love Him.

_____

_____

It's important to remember that His plans for you will be different than those for your best friend. So stop comparing yourself. You are a one-of-a-kind masterpiece. Ask God to help you see yourself that way.

Pray about it: If you struggle with seeing yourself as the treasure you are, commit to praying about it. You may want to pray back to God such scriptures as Psalm 139. The more you saturate your mind with the truth, the more you will see yourself for the unique creation you are.

✔ **Try This:** Find a recent picture of yourself and attach it to the center of a big piece of paper. Next, on the paper write your positive traits and abilities. You may want to include such info as you are a good listener (and draw an arrow to your ears) or that you have a great sense of humor. You can also include positive comments about your appearance. For instance, you may have strong arms, straight teeth, or shiny hair. Lastly, include some Bible verses that explain how special you are to God. You can include some from this lesson or look for others. The next time you have a bad hair day, let this picture remind you that you are a handmade treasure.

✝ **Living the Word:** Read Jeremiah 29:11.

• According to this verse, describe the plans God has for you.

_____

_____

• What steps will you take to help you remember that you are God's masterpiece created with a special plan for your life? _____

_____

_____

• Write a prayer thanking God for making you the way you are. Next, ask Him to use you in your generation to fulfill the purpose He has for you. _____

_____

_____

_____

_____

_____

It's time to open up the closet, dig out that dirty laundry, and bring it to our "cleanser," Jesus Christ.

But if we confess our sins to him, he is faithful and just to forgive us and to cleanse us from every wrong.
1 John 1:9 NLT

Dirty Laundry

My closet is the last thing I would want you to see if you came to my house. It's the place I throw all of the stuff I don't want to deal with at the moment. Unfortunately, that's how I sometimes deal with the closet of my life.

From the time I was a little girl, neatness has not come naturally to me. The biggest arguments with my mother were over cleaning my room. I totally hated it. Cleaning took work, and my sanguine personality liked to play. So when I lost the battle and had to clean my room, the closet became the junk pile. I crammed so much stuff into my closet that I would have to shove the door closed with all my might. Well, I'm sure you can imagine what happened when my mom decided to put her life at risk by opening my closet door. *Avalanche!* Everything came tumbling out, and my room was messier than ever.

Closet Confessions

By looking at a CD cover or one of our posters, you might not know that I am a messy person. I try to look as good as I can. But I can definitely say that I have dirty laundry in the corners of my closet. And when I don't deal with it, things begin to stink. It's the same with my heart. When I don't deal with the troublesome issues in my life, my aroma is less like a rose and more like a clove of garlic. See if you identify with any of the "dirty laundry" I have stuffed back in my closet.

Closet Comparisons

One of the issues that piles up in the closet of my heart is *comparison*. For some reason, other people's closets always look better than mine. I end up making all kinds of assumptions about what others have in their closets. I assume they have it more together than I do, that their clothes are cuter than mine, that everything is in perfect style, and that everything fits perfectly.

You would think that I would have outgrown comparisons by now, but all that has changed is what I compare. In high school I thought, *She's prettier, skinnier, smarter, a better singer, or a better athlete than I am*. Now as an adult I think, *She's a better mom, she's a better wife, she has it all together, or she's more spiritual than I am*. Then there are the never-ending comparisons: *She's skinnier, has less cellulite, or has less wrinkles. How is it possible that she has had four kids and still looks amazing?*

Here's the problem. When I compare myself to someone else, I'm discontent with who I am and what I have. And as we said in the last chapter, God has made you who you are on purpose and for His purpose.

God does not intend for you to compare yourself to others; He intends that you look at yourself objectively, in light of who He has created you to be: "Each person should judge his own actions and not compare himself with others. Then he can be proud for what he himself has done" (Galatians 6:4 NCV).

The Bible actually says that you are a *masterpiece*! You are who God intended you to be! He wants you to be you—not someone else. "For we are God's masterpiece. He has created us anew in Christ Jesus, so that we can do the good things he planned for us long ago" (Ephesians 2:10 NLT). God had wonderful plans for you—plans that He began before you were even born.

Closet Fear

Fear is another one of those issues that I cram inside my closet, hoping it will just go away. When I was in the ninth grade, I had an experience that I allowed to affect me for years. I air-balled a game-winning free throw to lose against our rival team in basketball. I thought my heart was going to explode and never recover. But the next day at school, I put on my happy-girl smile and acted as if everything was fine. Yet from that point on, with every free throw, I lived in fear that I would miss again. Well, more often than not, I did miss, because I never let myself get past that moment.

Basically, I became a poor loser. You see, when I missed a shot, I would say to myself, "You stupid idiot, you knew you would miss that shot. You never should have played basketball in the first place. Next time you had better make it." Well, with that kind of attitude, do you think I made it?

Instead, I should have said to myself, "Although I don't like it when I miss, I realize that I can't make every shot. I noticed that my elbow wasn't in and that I didn't follow through my shot, so I'll practice those techniques this week and come to the game next week with more confidence." Then all next week, I should've stayed after practice a little and worked on my shot instead of grumbling to myself about what a loser I was.

To add to the messages in my own head, one of my coaches told me that I just couldn't "finish" and that I was a "choker." I made the mistake of believing her, and I even applied her words to other areas in my life— including my singing. When it was time for a solo, I lived in fear that I would mess up or crack on the most important part. Even today I struggle with that fear and have to keep turning it over to the Lord.

But as I grow as a Christian, I'm learning that the cure to fear is *trust*. Psalm 56:3 says, "When I am afraid, I will trust in you," and Isaiah 50:10 says, "Let him who walks in the dark, who has no light, trust in the name of the LORD and rely on his God." Those verses are worth memorizing! Get yourself a couple of three-by-five note cards and write these verses on them. Tape them to your mirror so you'll see them while you're getting ready in the morning. Repeat them until they are embedded in your heart. Next time you feel afraid or as if you are walking alone in the dark, remember the words to these verses and replace fear with trust.

Closet Pleaser

Being a people pleaser is another one of those "dirty laundry" issues that stinks up my closet. I didn't realize until a few years ago how much I was afraid of what people thought of me. Every decision and action I made was based on what people would think. When I came out of my closet in the mornings, I would put on a big smile and bubbly personality—whether I felt like it or not.

Where did we get the idea that Christians are always happy and doing great? I remember as a child having huge fights in the car on the way to church and then stepping into the parking lot and being all, "Great, how are you doing?" Do you relate?

Why is keeping up appearances so important to us, anyway? I guess it's because we want to fit in, we want everyone to like us, and we don't think they'll like us if we let them see our pain. So when we hurt, we slap a smile on our faces and pretend that everything is fine. And on top of that, we have the mistaken idea that as Christians, we have the responsibility to always appear joyful and happy.

But I now realize that being vulnerable to others and allowing them to see that I, too, have bad days gives them permission to share their pain with me.

And as I am open about my struggles, I can share about my Friend, Jesus, who stays by my side through it all. When I am humble enough to share the real me, I can share my need for a real Savior.

In her book *Deceived by Shame, Desired by God*, Cynthia Spell Humbert says this, "To admit that we have needs is not an admission of weakness, it's a confession of our humanity, we all have needs . . . that's the way God made us . . . and to admit that we have needs is not only truthful, it's beneficial."[1]

Closet Secrets

At every Girls of Grace conference, we get questions from girls who are struggling with deep, dark secrets. Sadly, these girls often hold their pain inside because they are afraid to ask for help. Let's take a closer look at these secrets.

No Fault of Your Own

Some of our dirty laundry is a result of what other people do to us and is no fault of our own. Some families hide awful secrets—alcoholism, sexual abuse, verbal abuse, or neglect. I can't speak from experience on this kind of secret pain, but I'd like you to hear the story of a friend of mine who can:

> I was abused by my father sexually, physically, and verbally for seven years. His abuse broke my heart, distorted my view of male authority figures and of God, and shaped my self-image into a victim mentality. I never told anyone about the abuse during those seven years; I even held the secret in

many years after. Holding this family secret caused much pain, which led to an eating disorder, severe depression, low self-image (suicidal thoughts), and a sexual addiction.

At the age of twenty-eight, I finally shined the light of truth on the dark secret that had bound me in chains for so many years. I finally found the courage to seek help and tell the truth. Now I'm learning to live in the light, and through counseling I've learned to talk about the pain I encountered. In doing this and in looking to the Author of my life, I now stand in victory—free of shame, guilt, and anger.

When I look back at those years of abuse, I wish I had told the secret—no matter what happened afterward. So this is my advice to you: if you have a secret like this, run and tell it to someone you trust, someone who can help you get out of the situation! Don't hold your secret in. Go to a teacher or pastor or counselor—someone who can help you.

Even though life has been a long road with much pain, confusion, and simply wondering, *why me?* I have learned that the journey is not a sprint, but rather a marathon that I have to keep training for. I have also learned that life comes in seasons of dry times, sunshine, fun times, and down times. These seasons still come, but in each season, God molds me into who He is calling me to be. I am learning to see God's picture in full color and large screen, for He has created me for a purpose to do, say, be, and live for Him.

I have cried many hours, but I now know that God is always there watching, waiting, and catching every tear. I now see God as my loving father. His love has healed my heart, captured my heart, and has given me a beat that now beats after Him!

I'm proud of my friend for sharing her story and proud of her for finally getting help. I hope you heard her loud and clear when she advised those who are victims of abuse to seek out someone they can trust and ask for help. Even though I have no personal knowledge of this kind of abuse, I do know that it is *not* your fault. If you are a victim of abuse, you are not responsible!

But the abuse will not go away until it is brought into the light. The dirty laundry will continue to pile up, and the stench and the filth will grow until you are desperate for relief. And when we're desperate, we will try anything in the hopes of making life better—if just for one moment. But the actions we think will bring relief often only heap more harm upon ourselves. This "relief" may come in the form of drinking, cutting, drugs, sex, or eating disorders. All of which will lead to *avalanche*! Get help now.

The Result of Our Own Choices

We've talked about closet secrets that are totally outside our control, but there are some closet secrets that are the result of our own choices. And sometimes what starts out as a conscious choice spirals into addictions or entrapping behaviors that we *want* to get out of but feel we can't. You might be hiding a secret addiction to alcohol or drugs, or you might be entrapped in cutting, an eating disorder, or wrong sexual behavior. It's possible to hide an addiction to alcohol or drugs for a while, but eventually their power over you can severely affect your everyday life. You can hide an eating disorder for a while—until you are so sick that you need medical attention. And you can cut yourself for a while without anyone noticing, but this kind of secret is hard to keep. Cutting may seem to dull your inner pain temporarily; but eventually, you find that it no longer works. All of these secrets can lead to extreme danger and dysfunction.

Whatever problems our choices get us into, God has provided a way out. Scripture makes this promise: "The temptations that come into your life are no different from what others experience. And God is faithful. He will keep the temptation from becoming so strong that you can't stand up against it. When you are tempted, he will show you a way out so that you will not give in to it" (1 Corinthians 10:13 NLT). What an amazing promise! Whatever temptation you may be experiencing, God has promised a way out. This promise does a couple of things: on the one hand, it gives me tremendous hope; and on the other hand, it takes away my excuses.

Just like we make choices to begin harmful behavior, we can make choices to stop. Oh, I'm not saying that it's easy. It's not. It may be the fight of your life. But *choice* is one of the greatest blessings we have from God. Just like so many other gifts, we can use it for good or bad. Let's talk a minute about how you can use it to get help.

Getting Help

Just like there are stains in our clothing that won't come out in the washing machine—stains that require a professional dry cleaner—there are some problems in our lives that require professional help. There is no shame in getting help from a professional. Just as we go to medical doctors when we are physically sick, we should go to someone who can help when we are spiritually or emotionally sick.

But you can't get help until you are ready to tell someone that you need help. Talk to a trusted adult, a school counselor, a teacher, or other school official. If the first adult you talk to does not get you help, then go to another adult until you find someone to listen and to help you. You have the right to tell someone, and you have the right to expect help in getting this behavior stopped.

The most significant help we can ever get—whether our secrets are large or small—is found in the blood of Jesus. Only His blood can completely wash away the stains of our hurts, addictions, struggles, and sin. These words from one of my favorite hymns say it all:

Dirty Laundry

What can wash away my sins?
Nothing but the blood of Jesus.
What can make me whole again?
Nothing but the blood of Jesus.
Oh precious is the flow
That makes me white as snow.
No other fount I know.
Nothing but the blood of Jesus.

"If we walk in the light, as he is in the light, we have fellowship with one another, and the blood of Jesus, his Son, purifies us from all sin" (1 John 1:7).

It's time to open up the closet and, with His help and the help of someone who can walk with you, dig out that dirty laundry and bring it to our "cleanser," Jesus Christ. He is the only one who can truly begin the healing process. Don't you think it's time for the "stink" to go away?

STUDY
GUIDE

I Am a Masterpiece

📖 **Opening Scripture:** Ask God to teach you His truth today as you study His Word. Read Ephesians 2:10.

⭐ **Who You Are According to God:** If I were to ask you to describe yourself, what would you say? Would you say you are funny? Pretty? Smart? Mischievous? While many things would come to your mind, I doubt the word *masterpiece* would. When we run the tapes in our heads that tell us who we are, we too often tend to focus on the negative. We think of how we have a scar on our cheek or how we wish our hair were lighter or our hips thinner. We list the things we would change about ourselves. But if you were to ask God to describe you, do you know what He would say? Read on and see.

Fill in the blanks: Reread Ephesians 2:10 and fill in the missing words.

"For _____ are God's _____, _____ in Christ Jesus to do _____ works, which God prepared in _____ for _____ to _____."

What do you think? God's Word calls you His workmanship. Another way to say that would be you are His work of art. How does that make you feel?

- ❏ It makes me feel like a treasure.
- ❏ I don't feel anything because I can't believe it.
- ❏ It makes me want to see myself the way God sees me.
- ❏ _____

I Am a Masterpiece

Think about it: We have all struggled with seeing ourselves as His masterpieces. Why do you think it's so hard to believe what God's Word says about us? _____

_____

_____

⭐ **Looking at Everyone but Him:** One reason we find it so hard to trust what God's Word says about us is true is that we continually look at others rather than at God. We've all done it. We find someone that we think is nearly perfect and think of all the ways she is better, thinner, smarter, and more "together" than we are. This kind of thinking takes our focus off of where it should be: on God and His purposes for our lives.

What's your experience? Think of a time when you compared yourself to someone else? What was the result? _____

_____

_____

What does the Word say? Read Galatians 6:4. What does this verse teach about comparing ourselves to others?

- ❑ It helps us feel better about ourselves.
- ❑ It gives us something to do when we're bored in class.
- ❑ God warns us against it.
- ❑ It's not that bad as long as you don't say it out loud.

Pray about it: Maybe you are realizing that comparison robs you of seeing yourself as the masterpiece He has made you to be. If so, take some time to pray that God would help you view yourself the way He sees you. You might want to memorize Ephesians 2:10 and pray that back to Him each time you feel tempted to compare yourself to others. The comparison habit won't go away overnight, but as you pray about it daily, you'll find that you're more likely to look at Him than at everybody else.

Fear Factor: Maybe you, like Denise, have struggled with fear. It seems that our world offers up many fears for us to choose from: fear of failing, fear of what other people think, and fear of the unknown.

What's your experience? What are some of your biggest fears? (It's okay. Don't be afraid to list them. Admitting you have fear is the first step to freedom. _____

_____

_____

What does it mean? Read Proverbs 18:10. What does this passage teach about the protection of the righteous when they come to God? _____

_____

_____

Think about it: The next time you find yourself wrestling with fear, look for a Bible verse that talks about trusting God. Read and memorize it. Then when fear pops its ugly head again, you will have the verse ready to pull out as ammunition. You can tell God that you have fearful thoughts and ask Him for the grace to trust Him through the situation.

I Am a Masterpiece

⭐ **"What Do They Think About Me?"** We've all been there. We walk into a room and wonder what everyone is thinking about us. (Most of the time, they aren't thinking of us at all, because they are thinking of themselves.) We are having a sad day; and when someone asks us how we are, we lie. We want to please people. We want to have a certain image, and what we say and do is determined by what will make others like us. While there is nothing wrong with wanting others to like us, our desire to please people shouldn't drive how we live. Pleasing God should be light years more important to us than pleasing other people. So why is it often the other way around?

What's your experience? Have you ever let the fear of what others think about you change your behavior? If so, explain._____

_____

_____

What does it mean? Read Proverbs 29:25. What do you think this passage means by "a snare"?_____

_____

_____

Instead of looking to other people, whom does this verse point to as trustworthy?_____

Think about it: Do you want to be a God pleaser or a people pleaser? You'll probably need to make this decision every day. Maybe even every hour or minute. Determine that as His masterpiece, you will let God, not the world, determine who you become.

☆ **Let God Set You Free:** As you give over comparisons, fear, and people pleasing to God, you'll find it's easier to see yourself as the masterpiece He created. Maybe you have other things that hinder you from living as His one-of-a-kind work of art. There may be hurts and painful memories that you have never shared with anyone. Maybe you have an addictive habit, such as an eating disorder or cutting, that holds you back from seeing yourself as His treasure. Whatever it is, God can set you free. Come to Him honestly today, and let Him begin the process of freeing you from the inside out.

What does the Word say? Read John 8:32. When we live by God's truth, what is the result? _____

What do you think? Are there areas in your life where you need God to set you free? If so, list some of them here. _____

_____

_____

✔ **Try This:** It's important to have people in our lives whom we can trust with private and often painful information. Make a list of some people whom you could confide in and who would treat what you share with great care and respect. If you can't think of anyone, put down the name of a youth leader, pastor, or teacher you know. _____

_____

I Am a Masterpiece

✝ **Living the Word:** Read James 5:16.

• What does this passage say we should do with others? _____

_____

_____

• What will the result be? _____

_____

_____

• What does James 5:16 say about prayer? _____

_____

_____

• Will you ask someone to pray with you that you will start to see yourself as His loved and special masterpiece? If so, list her name here.

_____

• If you have suffered some form of abuse and have never told anyone, this Bible study was written just for you. Look at the list of trustworthy people you made, and choose one person to tell today. If it is literally impossible to tell that person today, determine to do it tomorrow. Letting someone know what happened to you is the first step to healing. Will you take that step to get help today? _____

If we truly want to have the closet of our hearts designed by the great Creator, Organizer, and Finisher, we must spend time with Him.

So get rid of all the filth and evil in your lives, and humbly accept the message God has planted in your hearts, for it is strong enough to save your souls.

James 1:21 NLT

Closets by Design

One day I came home from a trip, and my husband had several brochures lying on the table. No, they weren't brochures of Hawaii, the Caribbean, or the Bahamas. They were brochures from interior closet designers. Sound exciting? Not really. But necessary. Stu had been at home a few days too long with my kids while I was on the road and had gotten tired of the mess.

Stu is the choleric personality—the one who is in control, likes organization, and is goal oriented—and he had a goal in mind: to organize our closet. Ugh! I'd rather just go get ice cream and forget about it. But I reluctantly set some meetings with different designers, and we decided to go with Closets by Design.

Deborah was a very nice lady—enthusiastic and energetic. She made me feel as if this would be an easy and fun task. We talked about my lifestyle— the need for easy packing and unpacking, what clothes I wore the most, and the easiest setup for putting things back where they belong. She then began to draw out what she felt would best fit our needs. We agreed on a plan, and they went to work. Finally the shelves were built and rods put up. Eventually the bill was paid, and Deborah was gone.

There was only one problem. Now I had to organize all of my things and put them back in the closet. Where was my enthusiastic cheerleader now? I was left to deal with all the "stuff." Thankfully, I have very organized friends who gave me some great tips. Some of these tips may come in handy for you, too.

1. *Separate your clothes into pieces you want to keep and pieces you don't.* I had to go through my clothes, piece by piece, and figure out what fit, what didn't, what looked good on me, what didn't, what had stains that weren't going away, what needed alterations, and what couldn't be fixed. Then there were the shoes that I had to decide if they were in style or not. Was it okay to get rid of an old Point of Grace outfit? All of those questions.

2. *Divide the "don't keep" pile into "throwaway" and "giveaway" piles.*

3. *Divide the "keep" items into sections: pants, jeans, skirts, boots, heels, etc.*

4. *Put everything into the closet accordingly.*

5. *Add pieces to make wardrobe complete.* This was my favorite part, by far!

Understand that this was an extreme task for me. None of it came easy, and I didn't consider it a fun pastime. I could only bear it because of what my husband promised I could do if I completed this task: he said I could go shopping and add to what I had to complete my wardrobe!

Well, I have to tell you what a wonderful feeling I had when it was all done. I realize that it will take work for me to keep it clean, and we will see how long it lasts; but hopefully I have learned that it's much better to deal with things at the moment than to let them build up.

Now, how does this fit in with your own closet and your story? Let's see.

Take a Personal Inventory

Just like you sometimes take an inventory of your closet and get rid of the crummy, outdated stuff, you can take a personal inventory of yourself and take away some of the bad and add some good. Here are some ideas of how to go about making your life a "Closet by Design."

Step 1: Remember That You Are Designed by God

"The LORD who created you says: 'Do not be afraid, for I have ransomed you. I have called you by name; you are mine'" (Isaiah 43:1 NLT). God is the one who shaped you. He knows everything there is to know about you and has designed you with purpose. People and circumstances have added to the original design and made it a little messy, but God's plan for you is still intact. There's a big difference in my closet organizer, Deborah, and God. God not only designed your closet, but He will be the friend who helps you inventory, clean, and continue to grow the wonderful you He designed you to be.

Step 2: Figure Out What's Within Your Control and What's Not

We waste all kinds of energy and emotion trying to change things that are totally beyond our control. We can't control our family, the circumstances we were born into, how tall we are, or the skin type we have. We can't change our basic personality type or the gifts and skills we were born with. But there are a *lot* of things we can control. So let's get to work.

Step 3: Make a List of What You Like about Yourself

Go back to my chapter titled "If the Shoe Fits, Wear It," and review the SHAPE section. List the things about the SHAPE God gave you that are good. Don't stop with the first things that come to your mind. Spend some time on this point, and write down at least five positive qualities about yourself.

Step 4: Grow the Gifts God Has Given You

Making the list in step three is just the beginning. Growing in the gifts God has given you is the next step. Beside each thing you like about yourself, write the first action step you will take to develop and grow in that attribute. Know that God will actively work in you to help you grow: "Being confident of this, that he who began a good work in you will carry it on to completion until the day of Christ Jesus" (Philippians 1:6).

Step 5: Make a List of Things You Want to "Throw Out" of Your Inner Closet

Be honest but not brutal. Some people have a hard time seeing their own faults, while others can see little but their faults. This is not a time for either extreme. Take an honest, objective look at yourself, but don't tear yourself apart.

Remember that most of the junk in our closets is not the huge things, but little stuff that just piles up—stuff like jealousy, greed, selfishness, bitterness, and pride. I was convinced as I read in Matthew 23:25–26, where Jesus says to the Pharisees, "You hypocrites! You clean the outside of the cup and dish, but inside they are full of greed and self-indulgence. . . . First clean the inside of the cup and dish, and then the outside also will be clean." We've got to take the time to work on our hearts from the inside out.

Step 6: Take Action

Beside each "throwaway" item, write the first action step you will take toward change. For me, people pleasing was something that took up way too much space in my closet. Being a people pleaser was on my throwaway list. I'm learning that it's okay to say no to some things. I don't have to be on every committee or sign-up sheet that goes around. If someone is disappointed in me for declining a certain activity, I just have to know that I've prayed about what I'm to be involved in.

As we make commitments to change and decide on action steps, it is comforting to remember how very gracious and forgiving God is toward all the junk in our lives: "He does not treat us as our sins deserve or repay us according to our iniquities. For as high as the heavens are above the earth, so great is his love for those who fear him; as far as the east is from the west, so far has he removed our transgressions from us" (Psalm 103:10–12). And Isaiah 30:19 says, "How gracious he will be when you cry for help! As soon as he hears, he will answer you."

Step 7: Circle Items That Require Extra Help

Circle any items on your "throwaway" list that you don't think you can throw away by yourself. As we discussed in my second chapter, "Dirty Laundry," there are times when professional help is required. If you're having a hard time taking that step and getting help, take your fears and hesitations to God in prayer. Ask Him for guidance and wisdom.

There are certain things in our lives that, although we know they are bad for us, we have a hard time letting go of. Even things that are bad for us can, in some way, make us feel comfortable or secure. But as we grow in our relationship with the Savior, we have to let go of the harmful things that linger in the dark corners of our lives. Bringing the light of outside help into the dark can be an adjustment, especially if it is a sudden bright light. But God has chosen you as His royal princess, and he has called you out of darkness and into his light. "You are a chosen people, a royal priesthood, a holy nation, a people belonging to God, that you may declare the praises of him who called you out of darkness into his wonderful light" (1 Peter 2:9).

Bring in the New

No matter what we have in our past—and I mean no matter *what*!—God's unfailing love allows us to start fresh and new: "The unfailing love of the LORD never ends! By his mercies we have been kept from complete destruction. Great is his faithfulness; his mercies begin afresh each day" (Lamentations 3:22–23 NLT).

And with God's new mercies come the opportunity to be a brand-new person: "Therefore, if anyone is in Christ, he is a new creation; the old has gone, the new has come!" (2 Corinthians 5:17).

Becoming new is a process! When we ask God to change us in ways that please Him, He will do good and wonderful things. He will put new things in our lives every day: "love, joy, peace, patience, kindness, goodness, faithfulness, gentleness, and self-control"—the fruit of the Holy Spirit who lives in us (Galatians 5:22–23). These are the things that begin to make our SHAPE complete. The God "who began a good work in you will carry it on to completion until the day of Christ Jesus" (Philippians 1:6).

Here's the catch: if we truly want to have the closet of our hearts designed by the great Creator, Organizer, and Finisher, we must spend time with Him. Now that you've made this great start, stay in touch with God on a regular basis. It's that day-to-day cleanup that keeps us from getting back to the same old clutter. Why wait until you need another overhaul? Give Him a chance every day to show you where things should be put to make the most of your design.

You have the *best* Designer in the world. Trust Him! He will make all the difference.

STUDY GUIDE

Extreme Makeover

📖 **Opening Scripture:** Pray that God would speak to you in a specific way today as you study His Word. Then read Romans 8:29.

⭐ **Head-to-Toe Makeover:** Have you ever watched one of those makeover shows? You know, the ones where someone gets new teeth, new hair, cosmetic surgery, and a whole new wardrobe. You wouldn't even recognize these people if you were only shown "before" and "after" photos. Some of these makeovers give new meaning to the word *extreme*. Maybe when you watch shows like that, you think of all the things you would change about yourself. If you could, maybe you would change your nose or the color of your hair. If given the chance, most females would love a makeover. It's fun to get a new look and go from "before" to "after."

What do you think? Why do you think our culture is so infatuated with makeovers? _____

_____

If you could get one part of you "made over," what would it be? _____

_____

Did you know that God is in the extreme makeover business? He sees and loves the "before" you, but He has a great plan for the "after" you. He sees what you can become; and when you rely on Him, He can remake you with the ultimate extreme makeover.

Extreme Makeover

Fill in the blanks: Reread Romans 8:29 and fill in the missing words.

"For those God _____ he also predestined to be _____ to the _____ of his _____, that he might be the _____ among many brothers."

Think about it: God's end goal for what He wants you to be like isn't Jennifer Aniston, Hilary Duff, or even Billy Graham. Those goals are way too small. He wants you to be like His Son, Jesus Christ. He wants you to act like Him, love like Him, think like Him, and talk like Him. He wants you to be changed from the inside out.

☆ **A Good, Long Look in the Mirror:** Have you ever considered how many hours a week you spend in front of a mirror? If you're like most girls, you spend at least an hour or more looking in the mirror each day. There's the time when we dry our hair, pluck our eyebrows, and apply makeup. We stand in front of the mirror to style our hair and to evaluate our outfits. While there's nothing wrong with looking nice, it's important to remember that what's on the outside isn't the real us. It's just the shell we wear to live on the earth. So what mirror will the real me, not the shell I live in, look in?

What does the Word say? Read James 1:22–25. In this passage the Bible is compared to a mirror. According to verse 25, those who look at it intently gain what?

❏ Riches
❏ Freedom

❑ Fame

❑ Biblical knowledge

Reread verse 25. What does this verse promise will happen when we obey God's Word? _____

_____

Think about it: God's Word is the mirror for our spiritual life. When we look in it by reading, studying, and memorizing, we can see what God sees when He looks at us. God uses the Word to show us areas where we are doing well and others we need to change.

What's your experience? Describe a situation where God used a Bible verse or passage to show you something that He wanted you to change. _____

_____

_____

_____

Has there been a time when God used His Word to encourage you that you were on the right track? If so, describe that situation. ____

_____

_____

☆ **Change—From the Inside Out:** The problem with makeover shows is that they focus only on the outside person. No one ever talks about the real identity of the one they are making over. That's the difference between a God makeover and one that the world offers. God wants to make over the real you. He's interested in way more than the color of your hair or the shape of your eyebrows. He wants you to change from the inside out.

What does the Word say? Read Matthew 23:25–26. What do these verses teach about only taking care of our outer appearance and neglecting our hearts? _____

_____

_____

What do you think? Why do you think God is more interested in the inside of a person than the outside? _____

_____

_____

Are you more interested in your outer appearance or the condition of your heart? Explain your answer. _____

_____

_____

_____

⭐ **The Road to Change:** All of us have areas where we are growing and doing well. And we all have parts of our lives where we need God to radically change us. What are the steps to participating with God in His makeover process?

1. Prayer. If we're going to change, prayer is the first step. We need to humbly come before God, asking Him where He wants to change us.

Ask Him to show you where you are more like the world than Him.

Fill in the blanks: Read Psalm 139:23–24 and fill in the missing words. "_____ me, O God, and _____ my _____; _____ me and know my anxious _____. See if there is any _____ way in me, and lead me in the _____ everlasting."

Pray about it: You may want to pray this verse back to God when you start your quiet time each day. You can trust that if you ask Him to search your heart, He will. He will show you places in you that need to change. Instead of jealousy, He wants to form in you a generous and giving heart. Instead of pride, humility. Instead of selfishness, selflessness. Ask Him to reveal the places in your heart that need a makeover, and be prepared: He will answer you.

2. Renew your mind.

Since change comes from the inside out, it's crucial that your mind changes. What we think about determines what we'll become.

What do you think? How much "mind time" do you give to the things of God? _____

What does the Word say? Read Romans 12:2. What is the key to being transformed (changed)? _____

_____

_____

We renew our minds when we spend time looking into the Word of

Extreme Makeover

God, our spiritual mirror. The more we know the Word, the more our thoughts and hearts will look like Him. The more the inside changes, the more the outside will change, too.

✔ **Try This:** We renew our minds when we read, study, or memorize Scripture. What practical steps will you take to renew your mind this week? _____

_____

_____

Is there an activity that has a worldly influence on you that you need to replace with an activity that has a godly influence? If so, what is your action plan for change? _____

_____

_____

✝ **Living the Word:** Becoming conformed to the image of Jesus is a lifelong process. No one ever gets 100 percent there. But each day, as we determine to become less like the world and cooperate with Him, we'll become more like Jesus.

Read Philippians 1:6.

• Who is the "He" referred to in this verse? _____

• What promise do we find in Philippians 1:6?_____

_____

_____

• God promises to continue His makeover on you for the rest of your life. Aren't you thankful that He doesn't just leave us the way we are? Take a few moments to write a prayer thanking Him that He is working in you to make you more like His Son, Jesus.

_____

_____

_____

_____

_____

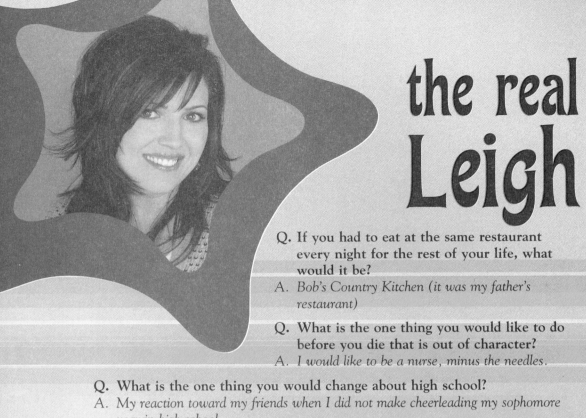

the real Leigh

Q. If you had to eat at the same restaurant every night for the rest of your life, what would it be?

A. *Bob's Country Kitchen (it was my father's restaurant)*

Q. What is the one thing you would like to do before you die that is out of character?

A. *I would like to be a nurse, minus the needles.*

Q. What is the one thing you would change about high school?

A. *My reaction toward my friends when I did not make cheerleading my sophomore year in high school.*

Q. What is the one material possession you would take from Denise?

A. *Her platinum diamond ring given by Word Records for Point of Grace's first platinum-selling record.*

Q. What characteristic do you love most about yourself?

A. *I have skinny legs.*

Q. What is the most embarrassing thing about yourself?

A. *I have a habit of belching in or out of public.*

Q. What is the one thing you tried out for and never made?

A. *I tried out for cheerleading my sophmore year in high school and did not make it. I was completely devastated!!*

the
games
girls play

A coach is one
who has gone before us—
someone who can
show us the way.

Without wise leadership, a nation falls;
with many counselors, there is safety.
Proverbs 11:14 NLT

Choosing a Great Coach

Life is kind of like a game, isn't it? In life we experience wins and losses. We learn the importance of teamwork and playing by the rules. And just like in a game of basketball or soccer, we find that if we want to win at the game of life, we can't just wait for the game to happen to us. We have to take control and be on the offensive. We have to develop game plans and make deliberate choices if we want to win.

In my three chapters, I want to talk with you about some of the choices you can make as you play the game of life. The first choice we'll talk about is who your coach will be. If you're on a sports team, you probably didn't get to choose your coach; but in the game of life, you get to choose. You don't have to settle for whoever life throws your way.

Why do you even need a coach? Why can't you just play this game of life on your own? Well, I suppose you could. And since we're talking about choices, I have to say, that whether or not to choose a life coach is up to you. But there are so many blessings to having someone older and wiser walk beside you and speak truth into your life as you make this sometimes-difficult journey. Let me share with you some of the reasons you might choose to have a coach/mentor as you live out the game of life.

Reasons to Choose a Coach

First, the Bible teaches the importance of listening to and learning from others. In Titus 2:4 Paul tells the older women to "train the younger women." The book of Proverbs also talks about the value of listening to the advice of others: "Listen to advice and accept instruction, and in the end you will be wise" (19:20), and "Without advice plans go wrong, but with many advisers they succeed" (15:22 GW). Throughout the Bible we are given example after example of how people, through their relationships with others, were taught, encouraged, and cautioned. The apostle Paul loved Timothy and delighted in teaching and "coaching" him. Mary's cousin Elizabeth brought her much comfort. And Ruth cherished and received all that Naomi, her mother-in-law, had to say. Ruth actually *appreciated* her advice. (How many of us appreciate the advice of others?)

Second, since older people have had more life experiences, they have wisdom that they have gained along the way—wisdom that can help you in what you are experiencing now. The game of life can put some pretty tough obstacles in our path, and the wisdom of someone who's been through a similar experience can help us make it through.

Choosing a Great Coach

A coach is one who has gone before us—someone who can show us the way. I was the baby in my family, and I would get so mad at my older sisters because they got to do things long before I did—like wearing makeup, dating, driving the car, and even sitting at the adult table for Thanksgiving dinner. But now as I look back on those memories, I realize that watching them go first provided an opportunity for me to learn from their experiences.

I was in my late twenties before I understood the value of a mentor. Now I am *passionate* about this topic, because I've seen what a blessing a mentor has been for my life. I want you to have the same blessings.

When I was twenty-seven, I began developing a relationship with a wonderful woman named Debbie Petersen. Over the years Debbie has become my mentor. Debbie and I discuss everything from fashion to forgiveness. She provides me a safe haven where I can be completely honest. I feel no hesitation at all in admitting my deepest feelings to her. Debbie does not judge me, but she listens to me with unconditional love. She prays with me and encourages me when life's challenges arise. She doesn't always have the answers, but she points me in the direction of the One who does. I can always count on her responses to be grounded with a godly perspective. I have found that receiving instruction and counsel in a loving manner from Debbie has made me a better person.

Qualities of a Coach Worth Following

But you can't let just anyone be your coach. You have to take the initiative and be in control. You have to be on the offensive and choose the right coach for your life. Here are some things you should look for in a coach.

A Great Coach Has a Plan of Action

Have you ever heard the saying "If you fail to plan, you plan to fail"? Your plan determines your destination—you can take that to the bank! My first vocal coach was a man named Mr. Rogers. Not the Mr. Rogers from PBS children's television, but a very sweet man all the same. Mr. Rogers's plan of action was to teach me how to sing correctly. The most difficult part in his plan was the fact that I had to *practice*! I have a friend whose prayer for wisdom was how I felt about practice: "Lord, help me to go to sleep and wake up wise, because I don't want to do the hard work!" Wouldn't it be great if it could happen that way? A great coach knows the importance of a plan of action and knows how to inspire you to do the work necessary to work that plan.

A Great Coach Calls You to Do Your Best

A good coach calls you to do your best even when that means pushing you to do more than you want to do. One particular time while I was in college, I came to a voice lesson so unprepared that my vocal coach asked me to leave and not come back if I wasn't going to take my lessons as seriously as he did. Talk about a cold splash of water in the face! And I needed it! My vocal coach had a passion and a love for teaching. Teaching not only brought him pleasure, he took pride in his students' progress. So when I didn't take his instruction seriously, my coach was insulted—and understandably so.

You know, God wants us to do our best, too. In the New Testament, the apostle Paul uses the phrase "more and more" in several places to encourage us to go beyond the good we are already doing and strive for the best: "This is my prayer: that your love may abound *more and more*" (Philippians 1:9). In 1 Thessalonians 4:1, he instructed the Christians in Thessalonica to "live in order to please God," and "to do this *more and more*." Then in 2 Thessalonians, he thanks God for them because their faith was growing *"more and more"* (1:3). When you're looking for a coach for your personal life, look for one who isn't afraid to challenge you to do *more and more*—to do your very best.

A Great Coach Knows the Value of Setting Goals

All through my college years and even before, I had had the dream of being onstage as a member of the group Truth. Years of voice lessons, studying music, and performing weekend after weekend finally paid off. I was three weeks away from graduating college when I was asked to audition. I never would have gotten the opportunity to audition if it hadn't been for the dedicated mentors and teachers who, along the way, had taught me the value of setting goals. Long story short, I was asked to join the group. Wow! I was completely blown away. This had been a goal of mine for six years, and it was finally becoming a reality.

There are some things in life that we *desire* but that are beyond our ability to attain. But *goals* are within our reach. There is a difference in goals and desires. A *goal* is something I want and have some ability to attain. A *desire* is something I want but have no ability to attain.

First Corinthians 15:58 tells us not to "let anyone move you off the foundation of your faith. Always excel in the work you do for the Lord. You know that the hard work you do for the Lord is not pointless" (GW).

Hebrews 12:1–2 urges us to run the race of life by focusing on the goal before us: "Run the race that lies ahead of us and never give up. We must focus on Jesus, the source and goal of our faith" (GW).

A great coach helps you set attainable goals and teaches you how to do the hard work needed to reach them.

Choosing the Right Coach for You

Are you up for the game of your life? Are you ready to begin your search for your life coach? Here are some tips on how to find the right coach for you.

First, You Pray

The first thing you do as you set out trying to choose the right coach for yourself is *pray*. Ask God for wisdom. Ask Him for eyes to see the right person. It may be someone you least expect. Ask Him for guidance and help. Then be patient and give Him time to work.

Qualities to Look For

The first rule of thumb is that your mentor needs to be a *woman*. Relationships with guys are great—as friends, as godly boyfriends, as brothers, fathers, uncles, etc.—but when it comes to choosing a *mentor*, girls of grace need to choose a woman. In a coach-mentor relationship, you share your heart, your hopes, your dreams, your fears. You want to be able to be open and honest—and you want to be able to talk about boys and your feelings about them. There's too much extra "chemistry" going on between a boy and girl to try to have a mentoring relationship with a male. And besides that, no one understands a girl like another *girl*!

Beyond choosing a female, choose someone who is spiritually grounded, trustworthy, respectable, honest, kind, older, and wiser.

Places to Look

Okay, now you know what kind of woman to look for, so where do you find such a person? You'll find a quality coach where quality people are. Your church is an excellent place to look for a coach. Look at Sunday school teachers, pastors' wives, or female youth pastors. You also might find a coach in your own family—an aunt, a trusted friend of the family, or even a grandmother. You might find someone at school—a trusted teacher, guidance counselor, or even a sports coach. The point is, hang around places where good things are going on and where good people are hanging out, and your chances of finding a quality coach will greatly increase.

How to Begin a Relationship with Your Coach

Many mentoring relationships just begin naturally because you are hanging out in good places with good people doing good things. But sometimes you have to take some initiative, especially when you are making your own choices and choosing your own mentor. Keep in mind that it may take a few "false starts" to find the right mentor for you. A "false start" is when you start out doing something but things just don't work out at first. False starts are often used as practice for the "real start." So don't be discouraged if your first couple of efforts don't work out.

When you find a woman whom you'd like to get to know a little better, pray some more. If, after prayer, you still feel good about pursuing the relationship, ask the woman if you can get together for a few minutes after church or after class. You could get together for a Coke, to pray, to study the Bible, to go shopping, to have lunch, or just to talk.

Find what's comfortable for you, and reach out. Don't be surprised if she's surprised. This may be new to her, too. Just be genuine, open, and not pushy. If your first attempt turns out to be a false start, get back on your knees, and pray some more. It's worth the effort!

Of course, the ultimate Coach is Jesus Christ. He loves you more than you can imagine, and He's always ready to begin a relationship with you at any time, anywhere. The choice is yours!

making it real

STUDY GUIDE

A Life Coach

📖 **Opening Scripture:** Begin today's study by reading Ruth 1:16. Ask God to speak to you in a specific way as you study His Word.

⭐ **What Kind of Coach?** Have you ever had a really great coach? You know, the kind who shows you how to reach down deep inside yourself and do your best? The kind who challenges you when you're slacking and applauds you when you find success? A good coach has a way of really bringing out the best in us. We do better when there is someone on the sidelines who has trained and encouraged us.

Maybe you don't play sports, so you've never had an actual coach. But you may have had coaches in your life who just weren't called coaches. Maybe your coach was a tutor, dance instructor, teacher, parent, or youth leader. Somehow this person always knew what to say to inspire you to do your best.

What's your experience? Who has been the best "coach" in your life? What have you learned from this person? _____

_____

_____

What does the Word say? In Ruth 1:16, Ruth is talking to the coach in her life, her mother-in-law, Naomi. After Ruth found herself a widow at a young age, she realized that she was going to need someone to help her and teach her.

A Life Coach

Reread Ruth 1:16. How serious is Ruth about following Naomi?

- ❏ She's totally kidding.
- ❏ She is very committed.
- ❏ She's not at all serious.
- ❏ She'll follow if it's convenient.

What do you think? Ruth found a coach and decided to pursue that relationship with all that she had. What about you? Have you ever found someone older than you who could coach you in your spiritual walk? If so, who is that person? _____

Think about it: While it's important to have many older, wiser people in our lives, it's essential to find one person in particular who can encourage us in our spiritual walks. This may be a youth leader or older woman who goes to your church. You'll want your primary coach to be a female, as she can understand more of what you're dealing with. Make sure that she has a strong walk with Jesus Christ. Is she someone you want to become like someday? Does she honor Christ in her choices? Is she someone your parents approve of?

☆ The Difference a Coach Makes

What does the Word say? Read Proverbs 19:20 and fill in the missing words.

"_____ to advice and _____ instruction, and in the end you will be _____."

The Games Girls Play—Study Guide

Did you catch it? When we listen to the coaches in our lives, what will the end result be? _____

What's your experience? Has there ever been a time in your life when you listened to a coach and were wiser because of it? Describe the situation.

_____

_____

What do you think? Read Hebrews 10:24–25. In what practical ways do you think having a coach could encourage you? _____

_____

_____

What does the Word say? Read Hebrews 3:13. What benefits does encouragement to one another bring?

- ❏ It makes us run a marathon.
- ❏ It keeps us from the consequences of sin.
- ❏ It makes us happy.
- ❏ There is no benefit.

God never intended for Christians to "go it alone." We all need people in our lives who help and support us as we follow after Him. The more people you have in your life who encourage you to pursue Him, the easier it will be to do so.

⭐ **Finding Your Life Coach:** Maybe you're thinking that you just don't know anyone who walks with Christ and would be willing to invest in your life. Well, don't be discouraged. Remember that God wants you to grow and that He is capable of sending someone to help that happen. There may be someone in your life already who you have just overlooked. Maybe you have an older relative who would be your coach. Or you could ask a youth leader from your church if she would be willing to do so.

Pray about it: Start praying daily that God brings you a lady to coach you in your spiritual walk. Keep your eyes open to whom He will bring. It may be someone you would have never expected.

Think about it: The best way to meet others who are following Christ is by going where those people hang out. If you are looking for a godly coach but you rarely attend church, you'll find that it is hard to meet one. Make sure you are putting yourself in positions where you can meet godly role models, and you'll be surprised at how many will just "pop" into your life.

What's your experience? Do you have a role model in your life who wholeheartedly supports your decision to walk with Christ? If so, who?

_____

_____

If you do, you may want to ask this person to be your coach. If not, keep praying and waiting. God will bring you someone in His timing. You may wonder what you will do once you and your coach agree to meet. First of all, get to know each other. You'll want to share a little bit about what you hope to get out of the relationship. Determine a time and place to meet, and decide what you'll do during that time. Maybe you'll study a book of the Bible or read and discuss a Christian book. Or you could just meet and discuss what God is teaching you both. Whatever you do during that time, you'll want to pray together. If you feel uncomfortable praying at first, just ask your coach to pray aloud, and you can pray silently.

✔ **Try This:** Read Philippians 2:1–2. Take a few minutes to write this verse somewhere you will see it each day. You may want to attach a sticky note to your computer screen or write it on your mirror. When you see the verse, work on committing it to memory. Pray that this verse would describe the relationship that you share with your coach.

✝ **Living the Word:** Reread Philippians 2:1–2.

• Verse 2 can be a good test to see if you and your coach are heading in the right direction. Do these characteristics describe your relationship? Are you like-minded in your decision to follow Christ? Do you have the same love for Him?_____

_____

_____

• Do you and your coach share the same purpose, to know Christ better? _____

_____

A Life Coach

• If you don't have a coach yet, what practical steps are you going to take to find one? _____

_____

• If you do have a coach, you may want to write her a thank-you note today telling her how much you appreciate her. It won't take long, and it will encourage her as she encourages you.

A cheerleader knows
how to find the positive
in the negativity of life
and invites us to
take a new look.

The heartfelt counsel of a friend
is as sweet as perfume.
Proverbs 27:9 NLT

Choosing a Cheerleader

As far back as I can remember, I wanted to be a cheerleader. I think the idea really took hold the year that Santa put pom-poms under the Christmas tree. We were your normal, middle-class family, but I had two older sisters—Dana and Reide—and our combined Christmas wish lists were pretty long; so our mom had to be financially creative when it came to choosing gifts for all of us. On one particular Christmas, Mom made all three girls a set of pom-poms. One set was red and white, another was green and white, and the third was green and yellow. I got the green and yellow set. *I loved them!* I was so excited and thrilled as I pretended to be a cheerleader.

From that early age, I've always valued the role of cheerleaders at any sporting event, and I've learned to value them in my personal life as well.

The chief role of a cheerleader is that of *encourager*.

A Cheerleader "Cheers" You On!

We all need a cheerleader as we play the game of life, because we all need encouragement from time to time. Life can be hard, and we need someone who can cheer us on and pick us up when we fall down. We need someone who can encourage us when we feel defeated. A cheerleader knows how to find the positive in the negativity of life and invites us to take a new look.

Barnabas, in Acts 9:26–15:39, was the apostle Paul's personal cheerleader. In fact, Barnabas's name means "son of encouragement"! After Paul's sudden conversion from being a killer of Christians to being a follower of Christ, the Christians in Jerusalem were afraid of him and wouldn't have anything to do with him—and understandably so. But Barnabas believed in Paul, took him around to the other believers, and convinced them to take him in. Barnabas's willingness to stand beside Paul resulted in a long-lasting, trusting relationship between the two men. Barnabas was a great help to Paul in his service and in teaching the gospel. And the rest is history—or, shall I say, the New Testament!

I, too, have had great encouragers in my life. One of those was my mom. One night when I was twelve years old, as my mother was driving us home after Wednesday night church service, we were talking about my singing abilities. The way I remember it, Mom simply said, "Leigh, you have a very special gift!" That's it. That's all she said. I don't recall the drive home, going to bed that night, or even the next morning; but I have *never* forgotten those words. My mom probably doesn't remember saying them, but her words encouraged me to stay in the game. Her "pom-poms" weren't green and yellow like mine; they were the colors of encouragement and enthusiasm.

I've already introduced you to another very special cheerleader in my life—my friend and mentor, Debbie Peterson. There are not enough trees in the forest to write all I have learned from her and her experiences. Talk about an encourager! She refuses to let me feel defeated. I love being around her. I hang on her every word; her wisdom infuses me! Debbie has an incredible testimony of God's redeeming love and mercy and is enthusiastic about sharing it with others. I look at her life and want to be more like her: she studies the Bible, is a prayer warrior, and takes time to invest in people's lives. Debbie understands her frailty as a human being and that without Christ she is nothing. Understanding that, she has a heart of compassion and not condemnation, which is her most beautiful characteristic. Debbie's very life encourages me to live better.

Think about the people in your life. Are any of them cheerleaders? Or do you hang around with people who discourage you and bring you down? Some of the people in our lives are put there by God for very specific purposes—like Barnabas was put into Paul's life to enable him to share the gospel with the world. Others, like my mom, are put into our lives by birth. We really have no choice about our parents, our brothers and sisters, and aunts and uncles. I was very blessed to have an encouraging mom, but not everyone is. But we do have a choice concerning many of the other people who are in our lives, like my friend Debbie.

Be a Cheerleader to Attract Cheerleader Friends

You've probably been told that the best way to find a friend is to be a friend. Well, the best way to find a cheerleader for your life is to be a cheerleader in the lives of others. Several verses in the Bible talk about encouragement, and these verses give us great insight into what makes a cheerleader-friend:

A Cheerleader Builds Up Others

"Encourage one another and build each other up" (1 Thessalonians 5:11).

To build someone up is the opposite of tearing her down or destroying her. Think about your conversations and the conversations of your friends. Do your words and actions tear people down, or do they build them up? How about the people around you? Do their words and actions make you feel like you are being taken apart brick by brick, or do they build you up and make you stronger and more complete? Depending on your answer, it may be time to make some new choices.

Nothing pleases God more than when you choose to please Him. If you ask for His help in making changes in your heart, behavior, speech—anything in your life—He will work with you. The changes won't happen overnight; but stick with Him, and He will work wonders in you.

Choosing a Cheerleader

And if you need to choose some new friends, bring this to God, too, and let Him help you with that. Sometimes you need to leave old friends behind completely, and sometimes you just need to add new friends, while keeping the old.

A Cheerleader Encourages Outbursts of Love and Good Deeds

"Think of ways to encourage one another to outbursts of love and good deeds" (Hebrews 10:24 NLT).

Wow! What a cool way to say that. I want to have "outbursts" of love and good deeds in my life. That sounds fun! When you're with your friends, what kind of behavior and words "burst" out of you? Are they motivated by love? Do they result in good deeds? If not, think about the choices you can make to become a better cheerleader and to choose the kinds of friends who will cheer you on to this kind of outburst.

A Cheerleader Assures Us of God's Grace—No Matter What!

"My purpose in writing is to encourage you and assure you that the grace of God is with you no matter what happens" (1 Peter 5:12 NLT).

I don't know a single person who doesn't need this assurance. I blow it daily, and daily I need to be assured of God's grace. I need to be reminded that He loves me—*no matter what!* Think about the "no matter whats" in your life. You know what I'm talking about. The words you said. The lie you told. The thing you did. The secret you are holding inside. You need a cheerleader in your life who will assure you that the grace of God is with you no matter what.

And you need to be the kind of cheerleader who assures other people the same.

Now, please don't get me wrong. This does not mean that God is okay with the wrong you did or that there won't be any consequences for our sin. God is *not* okay with our sin, and the consequences are real. But Jesus has paid the price, and as 1 John 1:7 says, "If we are living in the light of God's presence, just as Christ is, then we have fellowship with each other, and the blood of Jesus, his Son, cleanses us from every sin" (NLT).

But even more than the "no matter whats" that we do, this verse is talking about the "no matter whats" that happen to us. The people Peter was writing to were undergoing severe persecution, and Peter was assuring them that "no matter what" happened to them, they were not alone. God was with them, and His grace surrounded them. So no matter what happens to you, God is right beside you. He doesn't always take the pain away, but He cries with you.

Are you the kind of cheerleader friend who encourages others to look to God's grace when the "no matter whats" of life start pressing in? Do you have cheerleader friends who help you do the same? If you don't have those kinds of friends, the choice is up to you. Remember, be that kind of friend, and you will attract that kind of friend.

A Cheerleader Encourages Obedience to God's Teaching

"Teach these truths, Timothy, and encourage everyone to obey them" (1 Timothy 6:2 NLT).

Obey is not a popular word. In fact, breaking the rules and doing it your own way are much more popular today. But the best of friends hold the line when it comes to doing it God's way.

The thing about God's commands is that they are for our *good*. Why do you think God has told us (in no uncertain terms) that sex outside of marriage is wrong? It's not because He doesn't want us to have any fun, but because He has created us so that we long for the loving, committed relationship that only marriage can bring. Sex is the precious fragrance that gives marriage its sweetness. When we play with sex before the right time and in the wrong relationship, we spoil what God meant to be beautiful and special. And when married people break their promise to each other by having sex with someone outside their marriage, they bring so much hurt to themselves, their spouse, and to their children. All of this and much more are behind God's commands to keep sex inside of marriage. What I want you to see here is that all of God's rules and commands are for our good and benefit. They are not arbitrary.

A good cheerleader friend will encourage you to obey God's teachings, even when those teachings are hard, because she knows this is best for you.

And as you grow into this kind of cheerleader friend, you, too, will encourage others to obey God's truths.

These are just a few of the characteristics of a great cheerleader friend, but they'll get you started in your search for friends who will cheer you on and as you strive to become that kind of friend yourself!

The Gift of You!

I find it hard to believe that you were created just to go to school, play, shop, and then die. No, you were created for greater things. Among other things, you were created to bless others, and what greater blessing could you share than the blessing of yourself? Someone once said that we need three things each day: someone to love, something to do, and something to look forward to. As you give yourself to others as a cheerleader friend, besides blessing them, you will be fulfilling these three needs in yourself: you will be loving others, you will be doing good for others, and your days will be filled with purpose and be worth looking forward to.

With Jesus by your side as the perfect cheerleader, you can become a lifelong encourager of others. Are you ready to be a cheerleader friend? Are you prepared to make the choices needed to bring some cheerleader friends into your life? If your answer to these questions is yes, then get your pom-poms, and let's go!

Someone on the Sidelines

📖 **Opening Scripture:** Read 1 Thessalonians 5:11. Ask God to speak to you in a specific way as you study His Word today.

⭐ **Someone Calling Out Your Name:** Have you ever played on a team or taken part in a competition? If so, you know that one of the first things you do when you get on the field or the court is look for your "fans." Now, you aren't Tiger Woods, so you probably don't have a whole crowd watching your every move. But chances are, someone is in the stands there to watch you. It may be your mom or dad or even your best friend. That person sees when you score and even when you blow it! And every now and then, you may hear her call out your name above the crowd! "Go, Mary!" "Good job, Sue!" It's those cheers that give you the strength to push on through the last play. You know someone is rooting for you and watching your every victory, no matter how small.

What's your experience? Have you ever had the experience where someone you love came to watch you compete or perform? If so, how did it make you feel?_____

_____

_____

Maybe you have never had someone come to watch you. If so, how did you feel? _____

Someone on the Sidelines

_____

_____

What does the Word say? Reread 1 Thessalonians 5:11. How can you be a cheerleader in someone else's life and build them up?_____

_____

_____

What do you think? Why is it so important that we cheer for those whom God has put in our lives? _____

_____

_____

☆ **Finding a Cheerleader:** Maybe you can't think of a single person in your life who cheers you on. Maybe you feel so alone and that no one really cares about you. If so, remember that your ultimate cheerleader is God. He is there with you every second of every day. He watches you sleep, gives you each breath, and cares more for you than you even care about yourself. He is for you! He loves you beyond what you could ever dream. Ask Him to help you find a cheerleader, or several cheerleaders, who can physically express the love and care that He has for you.

Pray about it: Ask God to bring you a cheerleader to cheer for you. Pray that He would provide you with a friend or family member who will encourage you as you follow God. Now, be open to how He answers this prayer. Sometimes His answers don't look like what we think they will. They may not be who we thought they would be or come from the obvious places we would look, but God will answer your prayer. Be patient and open to His answer.

Think about it: One of the best ways to find a cheerleader is to be one. Who do you know who needs encouragement? Maybe there is someone in a class or in your family who needs to hear an uplifting word from you. Make sure that you take the opportunity to build this person up. You will not only help her, you will find that you are making a friend as well.

What does the Word say? Read Romans 15:1–2. What does this passage teach that our focus should be?

- ❑ Finding cheerleaders to encourage us
- ❑ Building other people up
- ❑ Having a lot of friends
- ❑ Telling others how to change

It's one of the ironies of life that when we focus on serving others, we find that our own needs are often met. When you look for others to encourage, you don't really have to look for those to encourage you. More than likely, they will just show up in your life.

What's your experience? Has there ever been a time when you made it a point to meet someone else's need and found out that you were encouraged in the process? If so, describe what happened. _____

Someone on the Sidelines

_____

_____

☆ Cheering with a Purpose

Fill in the blanks: Read 1 Samuel 23:16 and fill in the missing words.

"And Saul's son Jonathan went to _____ at Horesh and _____ him find _____ in God."

When we are looking for cheerleaders or wanting to be one in someone else's life, we need to remember that the purpose isn't just to make someone feel good. The purpose of a cheerleader is to point someone else to God.

What does the Word say? Reread 1 Samuel 23:16. What did Jonathan, David's cheerleader, do for him?_____

_____

_____

What does it mean? What are some practical ways we can do that for someone we are trying to encourage?_____

_____

_____

When you want to help someone else find strength in a tough time, it's important to point that person to God's character and His Word.

What do you think? When we encourage someone to remember God's character, we're reminding him or her of who God is and what He is like. How would this help someone going through a tough time?

_____

_____

What's your experience? God's Word is the ultimate pom-pom when encouraging others. Has there ever been a time when someone gave you a Bible verse that changed your perspective when you were having a hard time? If so, describe the situation. _____

_____

_____

_____

_____

✔ **Try This:** Read Hebrews 10:24. Have you ever really stopped to think about the influence you have with your friends? You can encourage them to do or say things just by your very presence in their lives. You can set an example in your family with your siblings and even your parents. The verse says you can spur someone else to do the right thing. By your example you can start a ripple effect of encouragement that can change your family, your school, your town, or your world.

Take some time to do just what this verse suggests: consider. Make a list of some ways that you can start a chain reaction of encouragement in your family. How can you cheer on others in your

Someone on the Sidelines

school? Don't be afraid to dream big! I know of someone who wrote a different Bible verse on the back window of his car each morning before school. Each person who saw him driving to school was encouraged by God's Word and reminded of God's love. That was fifteen years ago, and people I know still talk about it. You never know what effects your choices to encourage others will have. _____

_____

_____

✝ **Living the Word:** Read Philippians 2:3–5.

• Encouragement is less an action and more a lifestyle. In what ways can you daily consider others better than you? _____

_____

_____

• What do you think verse 3 means by "selfish ambition"? What are some ways to overcome acting this way? _____

_____

_____

• It just comes naturally to look out for our own interests. Make a list of several people in your life, then next to each name write one way you can focus on his or her interests. _____

_____

_____

_____

• Verse 5 sums up the definition of an encourager. Write out a prayer asking God to help you daily choose the attitude of Jesus. Ask Him to give you the strength to model His love and care for people._____

_____

_____

_____

_____

_____

_____

_____

The wise referee knows that her actions should complement her authority, not contradict it.

> *Hold on to instruction, do not let it go;*
> *guard it well, for it is your life.*
> Proverbs 4:13

Choosing to Follow a Referee

The colors of a referee's uniform leave no room for confusion. They're black and white with no gray area whatsoever. Interesting, don't you think? Indecision is *not* a quality of a referee.

Although referees are not the most popular people on the field, they are absolutely essential to any sports game—and they are essential to the game of life as well. Like a referee's uniform, the basics of the referee's job are also quite simple:

1. To bring trustworthy wisdom and understanding to the game

2. To enforce the rules and hold players accountable for their actions

3. To provide protective boundaries

In our rational moments, we can see the benefits of having a referee in our lives, but when we want to do something against the rules, we wish we could do away with the referee.

You probably already have several referees in your life: your parents, teachers, youth pastor, and coach. All of these people have been placed in a position of authority and are responsible to bring wisdom, enforce rules, and provide boundaries. You usually don't get to choose who your referees are, but you do get to choose whether or not you follow your referee's lead.

The Benefits of a Good Referee

Let's spend a few minutes thinking about the benefits of a good referee.

A Good Referee Brings Wisdom

Wisdom could be defined as an intelligent attitude toward the experiences of life. Mere *knowledge* is not the same as *wisdom*. Wisdom is knowing how to apply knowledge to make life work. The best kind of referee brings not only firm understanding of the rules of the game but also wisdom that has been gained from years of experience in seeing those rules applied and the game played.

The Bible says, "The LORD gives wisdom, and from his mouth come knowledge and understanding" (Proverbs 2:6) and, "A wise person will listen and continue to learn and an understanding person will gain direction" (Proverbs 1:5 GW). A truly good referee is grounded in God. This is *extremely* important; otherwise, his decisions and counsel will not be reliable.

Have you ever heard the saying "Don't do as I do, do as I say"? While growing up, I only heard it a couple of times at the most, and I never quite understood its meaning until much later. Just recently, I provided an example of this saying without intending to.

One day I was out on our patio deck helping my husband hang a birdhouse on our backyard fence. I had left the glass door open and the screen door pulled to, so I could hear and see our two-year-old daughter, Darby Mae. Darby saw me outside and asked, "Mommy, can I go outside, too?"

"No, Darby," I answered. "You need to have your shoes on, not just your socks." Darby got surprisingly upset. It took me a minute to realize that I was outside in my socks—without my shoes. What was I teaching her? I immediately apologized.

"Darby Mae, I am so sorry that I told you no. I didn't realize that Mommy was outside in just *her* socks. You can come outside, too." Darby Mae came outside, and that was that.

This simple story illustrates an important message: the wise referee knows that her actions should complement her authority, not contradict it. Wisdom comes with experience and practice, and we are blessed when we have referees in our lives who guide us with their wise understanding.

A Good Referee Enforces the Rules

When I was a teenager, I asked my mom if I could go to a party at my friend's house. Mom quickly responded with a firm, "No!" I persisted and pleaded and gave her every reason in the book as to why I should be allowed to go, and I told her how unfair she was being for *not* letting me go. Her final response was, "I am concerned that there will be things going on at that party that frankly, you should not be involved in." Shamefully, I confess that I found a way and went to the party without her permission, only to learn that she was absolutely correct in her assumptions. That party did *not* represent anything good.

Why do we have such a hard time accepting rules that are for our own good? It may have something to do with the fact that we live in a fallen world; and where humanity is, there is sin. This is not an excuse, by any means, to give up the fight. However, it reiterates the importance of having godly people in our lives to hold us accountable for the choices we make.

In reality, it's hard to force other people to do things they don't want to do. But a good referee does enforce the rules by imposing consequences when the rules are broken. Sometimes the referee doesn't have to impose the consequences; sometimes life brings about those consequences naturally. I remember a very painful example that may help you understand that rules are indeed for our benefit.

My sister Reide and I had been warned *not* to ride our motor bike while our parents were not home. One afternoon after school, my sister and I decided to go against that rule. Reide was driving while I was on the back. Well, we hit some gravel and crashed. It was a very nasty fall. Reide's leg was pinned and—we found out later—broken. I was so freaked out; I thought she was going to die. I still have a scar to remind me just how "lucky" we were that it ended in just a broken leg and a very skinned-up elbow. But I can assure you, we learned our lesson. While I didn't like these consequences, they were a firm reminder that there was a price to pay for broken rules.

Of course, there comes a time when a good referee has to step back and let the player make her own choices. I found a poem from an unknown author that reminds us of the limitations of even the best referees. I'll share part of it with you here:

It's Your Move, Daughter

I gave you life,
But I cannot live it for you.
I can teach you things,
But I cannot make you learn.

. . .

I can take you to church,
But I cannot make you believe.
I can teach you right from wrong,
But I can't always decide for you.

. . .

I can advise you about your friends,
But I cannot choose them for you.

The Games Girls Play—Leigh

I can teach you about sex,

But I cannot keep you pure.

I can tell you the facts of life,

But I can't build your reputation.

I can tell you about drink,

But I can't say NO for you.

I can warn you about drugs,

But I can't prevent you from using them.

. . .

I can teach you about Jesus,

But I cannot make Him your Savior.

I can teach you to obey,

But I cannot make Jesus your Lord.

A Good Referee Provides Protective Boundaries

When Adam and Eve were in the Garden of Eden, God set some very clear and definite boundaries: "The LORD God commanded the man. He said, 'You are free to eat from any tree in the garden. But you must never eat from the tree of the knowledge of good and evil because when you eat from it, you will certainly die'" (Genesis 2:16–17 GW).

The purpose of God's boundary was not to restrict Adam and Eve but to protect them. Adam and Eve had the freedom to obey or disobey God—just as we do. Adam and Eve chose to disobey God, and they lived with the

Choosing to Follow a Referee

consequences of their choice. Our choices have consequences, too. Knowing this up-front should help us make better choices and become more responsible.

The boundaries set up by good referees are for our benefit and protection. When we cross those boundaries, we end up in the danger zone and get into all kinds of trouble. Think of a time when you crossed the boundaries set up to protect you. What were the consequences? You may be thinking of time spent with a boyfriend or at a party. If we are wise, we'll learn from these experiences and choose to stay within God's boundaries next time.

Studies have been done on the behavior of elementary schoolchildren playing on the playground with and without a protective fence. When a fence was in place, the children played freely and happily. They used the whole playground—all the way up to the fence's edge. But when the fence was taken down, they became afraid and insecure and huddled in the center of the playground, staying far from the street, not enjoying the playground equipment. These children understood the benefits and protection offered by boundaries. They didn't see the fence as something that restricted their fun but as something that allowed them the *freedom* to play without fear within their bounds.

This is what God had in mind when He set boundaries in place for us. They are for our protection and safety, so that we can live our lives in freedom and joy within the protection of His bounds.

Choosing a Referee for Your Life

Once again, the choice is yours. God has placed people in your life who bring wisdom, enforce the rules, and provide protective boundaries. And as long as your referees are grounded in God's Word and follow Him, they are worthy of your respect. But I have to offer one word of caution here. Unfortunately, we live in a world where not everyone who sets himself up as an authority figure can be trusted. Just because a person in authority tells you to do something does not mean you should do it. Not everyone who makes and enforces rules is pleasing to God. If you have a "bad referee" in your life who is forcing things on you that you know are wrong, get help from another adult. If the first adult you talk with doesn't help you, keep going until you find someone who will.

Now, with that said, there are many wonderful referees out there who—though not perfect—are to be trusted and followed. This is where the "game of life" becomes even more challenging. *Trust* means taking control out of our own hands and giving it to another person. Just like those children trusted the fence to protect them from the dangers of the street, when you find the right referee, you have to trust that the rules he puts in place are for your good. When your mom or dad says you can't go to a party that they know is bad for you, they are doing it for your good—not to harm you or keep you from having fun. This is where trust comes in. Or if your youth pastor sets up boundaries for a trip the youth group is taking, out of respect and trust, you stay within those boundaries—partly because it's right to obey his authority and partly because you trust his judgment.

Of course, the ultimate referee that every one of us must submit to in our lives is Jesus Christ. He has all the qualities we've talked about here and much more.

Dive into the Game of Life!

As you dive into the game of life, make sure that you have around you the key members of your team. Diligently pursue a coach-mentor to guide and support you. Become an encouraging cheerleader friend so that you can attract such cheerleaders into your own life. And finally, learn the value of a good referee so you can be blessed by the boundaries he or she provides.

As we've said in our other chapters, the best team member you can have is Jesus Christ. When you choose Him as referee, you've chosen one who *always* has your best interests at heart and who *always* sets proper boundaries in place for your good.

So get ready to dive in! Put your feet to the starting line, get your bat in position, get ready for that free throw! The game of life is about to start, and you have been chosen by God to be an eternal winner!

STUDY GUIDE

Who Makes the Call?

📖 **Opening Scripture:** Pray that God would speak to you in a specific way today as you study His Word. Read Romans 13:1–2.

⭐ **Authority Given by God:** Do you remember when you were little and couldn't wait to grow up so no one would tell you what to do anymore? You, like me, may have thought that when you were older you would be your own boss. You would decide when to go to bed, get up, and when to clean your room. It's funny that the older we get, the more "bosses" we seem to have. We have teachers, our supervisor at work, youth leaders and pastors, parents, and even the government. No matter how old we are, there is always going to be someone in authority over us.

Think about it: Why do you think that we have more authority figures over us the older we get? _____

_____

_____

What do you think? In your own words, define the word *authority*, as you understand it. _____

_____

_____

What does the Word say? Reread Romans 13:1–2. According to this passage, where does authority come from?

Who Makes the Call?

❑ Man has made it up to keep order.

❑ God established it.

❑ People who want to have no fun dreamed it up.

❑ Parents invented it.

When we rebel against our authorities, what does verse 2 say we are really doing? _____

_____

What does this passage teach is the result? _____

_____

_____

What's your experience? Has there ever been a time when you rebelled against authority and suffered consequences for your actions? If so, describe the situation. _____

_____

_____

_____

☆ **Obeying Authority Means Obeying God:** When we honor the authorities God has placed in our lives, we are ultimately obeying Him. He's called us to obey those He has placed over us—with the only exception being if they ask us to do something hurtful or that goes against God's Word. We fool ourselves when we think we're obeying God but not honoring those referees He has put in our lives.

The Games Girls Play—Study Guide

Think about it: List the authority figures God has put in your life. You may know some of them personally; and others, like law enforcement officials, you may not. _____

_____

_____

What does the Word say? Read Ephesians 6:1–3. What does this passage command regarding our parents? _____

_____

_____

What promise does God make if we obey our parents?_____

_____

_____

Think about it: Did you include your parents on your list of authorities? Whether or not you did, they are your main authority in this season of your life. While you did not choose them, it's important to remember that God did. As a matter of fact, we don't get to choose many of our authorities, but we do get to choose our responses to them.

What do you think? If you had to give yourself a grade for how well you obey your parents, how would you score?

- ❑ A—Always obey
- ❑ B—Bad sometimes and good sometimes
- ❑ C—Could seriously improve

Who Makes the Call?

❏ D—Don't honor them at all

What's your experience? How well do you obey other authority figures in your life, such as teachers and your boss at work? _____

_____

_____

_____

⭐ **The Benefits of Authority:** Like all of God's gifts to us, He always has a reason. He hasn't put authority in our lives to make us miserable; rather, it is to benefit us. There are three obvious benefits to God-given authority.

1. You gain wisdom from others. Proverbs 13:10 says, "Wisdom is found in those who take advice." When we listen to those who have walked with God longer, we can learn from their experiences. Describe a situation where you learned a lesson from a referee God has put in your life. _____

_____

_____

_____

2. You learn the rules and are taught to follow them. Have you ever tried to play a game that had no rules? If so, how did it work? It probably was a disaster, because in order for a game to be fun for everyone, all players must abide by the rules. It's the same way with life. For cities, families, schools, or even nations to run properly, someone needs to make sure that everyone is playing by the rules. Has there been a time when a referee in your life corrected you because you were disobeying? If so, what good came out of it? _____

_____

3. You are protected by boundaries. Referees help us know the boundaries God has set up to protect us. They teach us what is appropriate and what can hurt us. When we obey our authorities, we don't have to worry about suffering consequences for our bad decisions. On the other hand, when we disobey them, we run the risk of getting hurt. What steps can you take to avoid hurtful consequences that result from choices you make? _____

_____

_____

_____

✔ **Try This:** Read Proverbs 19:20. Think of some of the referees God has put in your life. Now write down some ways that you can receive their advice and put it into practice. Maybe you will ask your mom and dad to go for ice cream or a long walk. While you're with them, ask them what they would do in a situation that you're dealing with at school or with a friend. Really listen to what they say. God has placed them in your life for a reason. Do you trust Him enough to obey the calls your referees make? _____

Who Makes the Call?

_____

_____

_____

_____

✝ **Living the Word:** Read Hebrews 13:17.

• What are we commanded to do in this passage? _____

_____

_____

• What responsibility has God given our referees? _____

_____

_____

• Have you made the job of your authorities a joy or a burden? Explain your answer. _____

_____

_____

_____

• Are there some changes you need to make in how you respond to the referees God has placed in your life? If so, write them here. _____

_____

_____

_____

_____

• Is there a referee you need to ask to forgive you for past behavior? If so, write his or her name here. Make a point to talk with that person today. _____

• When we disobey our authorities, we not only make it hard on them, but we also make it hard on us. Write a prayer asking God to help you be a blessing to those referees He has chosen for you. Remember, when you obey them, you obey Him. _____

_____

_____

_____

_____

_____

_____

the real Heather

Q. If you had to eat at the same restaurant every night for the rest of your life, what would it be?

A. Cracker Barrel.

Q. What is the one thing you would like to do before you die that is out of character?

A. I want to live in a foreign country and learn the native language.

Q. What is the one thing you would change about high school?

A. I would not let Lanna Taylor give me highlights the day of the prom, because it turned my hair bleach blond. Believe me, it did NOT look good.

Q. What is the one material possession you would take from Leigh?

A. Her Lagos ring (sterling silver diamond emerald cut with gold trim).

Q. What characteristic do you love most about yourself?

A. My green eyes. I got them from my mom.

Q. What is the most embarrassing thing about yourself?

A. I have to wear a clear Band-Aid on my left earlobe in order to wear an earring because my earlobe is spilt in two (thanks to the heavy earrings in the eighties).

Q. What is the one thing you tried out for and never made?

A. I competed in the Metropolitan Opera competition and did not place!

me: God's
mirror
to the world

Being created in the image of God means that we were created to *look* like God—not on the outside, but in our character and in our souls.

God created man in His own image,
in the image of God He created him;
male and female He created them.
Genesis 1:27 NASB

Reflections of a Better Me

"Mirror, mirror, on the wall . . ."

As girls, we've all stood in front of a mirror a time or two. And we all know what a mirror does—it reflects the image of whoever stands before it. Sometimes we like the image we see reflected there, and sometimes we don't. The kind of mirrors we look into reflect our *outside* image. But in my three chapters, I want to talk with you about a different kind of image and a different kind of reflection. The story of our image and our reflection begins . . . in the beginning.

A Different Kind of Creature

"In the beginning, God created . . ." The first chapter of Genesis tells us that God created our whole world. When He created the animals, it says that He created them "after their kind" (verses 24–25 NASB). But when it came time to create *humans*, we hear a different story. Adam and Eve were not simply created after their kind; they were created "in the image of God" (verse 27 NASB).

But not everyone understands the truth that humans are set apart from the rest of God's creation. I was sad to see this evidenced in one of my daughter's picture books. Ella is an animal lover. When the weather is nice, my husband, Brian, and I take her to the zoo at least once a week. Recently, Brian bought Ella a book about animals. Not only does the book have great information, it also has a lot of colorful pictures! Ella loves for her daddy to read this book to her and show her the pictures of just about every animal you can think of.

There is just one thing wrong with the book. The authors evidently believe that humans evolved from some lower animal species, because right in the middle of all the animal pictures is a picture of a human being. Apparently, the authors don't see a significant difference between a human being and an animal.

But as Christians, we know and believe that humans are indeed different from all the other creatures of the world. Let's look at what God said in the Bible: "Let Us make man in Our *image*, according to Our *likeness*" (Genesis 1:26 NASB). Out of all the creatures that God made, only one creature—humankind—was made in the image of God. Being created in the image of God means that we were created to *look* like God—not on the outside, but in our character and in our souls. The fact that human beings are made in the image of God means that we are, in a sense, like God. God created us so that we would reflect His image.

Image Malfunction

Unfortunately, not long after God created the first man and woman, the Bible tells us in Genesis 3 that Adam and Eve sinned against God. Did you catch that? Though they were created to be God's image bearers on earth, Adam and Eve chose disobedience and rebellion instead. Because of their sin, we human beings don't reflect God's image as fully as we did before the Fall. Our moral purity has been lost, and our character does not mirror God's holiness. Our speech no longer continually honors God, and our relationships are often controlled by selfishness rather than love. As commentator Wayne Grudem says, "We are less fully like God than we were before the entrance of sin" through Adam and Eve.[1] That is not a pretty picture, is it?

At this point I know what you may be thinking. *This must be the feel-bad chapter of the book. I picked up this book for what? So Heather can tell me how sinful I am?* Patience, please. Just bear with me. In order to understand and appreciate the good news that's coming, I have to share with you the unfortunate truth about our sin.

This reminds me of two summers ago when Brian, Ella, and I lived next door to an amusement park in Cincinnati, Ohio. Every night at 10:00 p.m., the park would shoot off fireworks. And every night Brian and I would forget they were coming; so when those fireworks exploded, we thought we were being bombed. But think about it: why did the park officials decide to have fireworks at 10:00 p.m. rather than 10:00 a.m.? I'm sure that 10:00 a.m. fireworks would have been easier on those living near the park. But of course, the reason the fireworks were set off at night was that only in the context of a darkened sky could onlookers appreciate the brilliance and grandeur of those beautiful, bright (and loud!) fireworks. In fact, you would have been hard-pressed even to see the fireworks in broad daylight.

In the same way, in order to understand the beauty and glory of God's marvelous grace, we have to see it in the context of the darkened sky of humankind's sinfulness. As writer Anthony Hoekema says, the bad news (or the dark sky) is that even though "fallen human beings still possess the gifts and capacities God has [given us] . . . they now use these gifts in sinful and disobedient ways"—doing things that grieve the heart of God.[2] Rather than fulfilling God's purpose in our lives, we use our abilities, talents, and spiritual gifts to pursue our own selfish agendas. Our God-imaging gifts and abilities were not destroyed by the Fall, but they were perverted. As Hoekema explains, the image of God is still in us, but it is "malfunctioning."[3]

The image of God in us needs to be renewed. And this brings us to the next part of the story—*the good news*!

Image Renewed

Along comes our Knight in shining armor, the Lord Jesus Christ. Jesus is the fireworks in the sin-darkened night. Colossians 1:15 says that He is the "image of the invisible God." Jesus so closely reflects God that He was able to say, "Anyone who has seen me has seen the Father" (John 14:9). Jesus, as the Son of God, is the mirror image of God.

And as the mirror image of God, Jesus solves one of our difficulties as we try to look like God. Our difficulty is this: God is *invisible*. We can't see God, so how can we reflect His image? That's where Jesus comes in. Jesus showed us in living color—in flesh and blood—what God looked like. So if we want to know what God *really* looks like, all we have to do is look at Jesus, the fairest of them all.

When we repent of our sins and trust Jesus as our Savior, we are completely renewed—becoming like Him, reflecting God's image! Before our renewal we used our God-imaging powers in wrong ways, but now we are enabled to use these powers in right ways. That is what Paul meant when he wrote that as Christians we have a new nature that is "being renewed in knowledge in the image of its Creator" (Colossians 3:10).

God's purpose in creating you and me in His image was fulfilled in Jesus Christ. So as we trust in Him, we can be assured that our sins will be forgiven and that our purpose and mission in being God's image bearers will be restored. In fact, it could be said that the goal of our salvation in Christ is to make us more and more like God, or more and more like Christ, who is the perfect image of God (see Romans 8:29). That is what sets us apart from all of God's other creatures; that is what is unique about humankind. And as we become more and more like God, the story of our image becomes clearer as we reflect our Creator.

Image Overhaul

📖 **Opening Scripture:** Pray that God would speak to you in a specific way today as you study His Word. Read Genesis 1:26–27.

⭐ **Created for a Purpose:** Have you ever wondered what on earth you're here for? I mean, you wake up in the morning, go to school, and the next day you do it all over again. Some days are exciting, and some days are just plain hard. At times we can get discouraged and forget that God made us for a reason. The day you were born, all those years ago, was a special day in God's book. He saw you take your first breath and hasn't taken His eyes off you since.

What's your experience? Have you ever felt that you were just a cosmic accident and that God had no purpose for your life? If so, explain how you felt. _____

_____

_____

What does the Word say? Reread Genesis 1:26–27. In whose image did God create you?

- ❏ Your parents
- ❏ A monkey
- ❏ His own
- ❏ Your own

Image Overhaul

It's pretty amazing that, just as Heather wrote, human beings were created altogether differently than the animals. While He did create your beloved family Fido or Fifi, animals are not created in His image. The Bible says only humans have the divine stamp "in God's image" on them.

Think about it: What does the fact that you were created in the image of God say about your worth? _____

_____

_____

⭐ **Human Rebellion:** The good news is that we were created by God and for God. The bad news is that humanity rebelled against the very Creator who gave them breath. You have probably heard the story about how Adam and Eve disobeyed the one command God gave them in the garden. Because of their choice we have all inherited the same sinful nature. Everyone who has ever lived has sinned. The only One who has lived a perfect, sinless life is Jesus Christ.

Fill in the blanks: Read Romans 3:23 and fill in the missing words.

"For _____ have _____ and fall short of the _____ of _____."

What does it mean? According to this verse, are you included as one who has fallen short? Explain your answer. _____

_____

_____

_____

Rebellion, otherwise known as sin, has a very serious penalty. Romans 6:23 says, "For the wages of sin is death." This is serious news; but luckily, the story doesn't end there. Read on.

★ **Good News!** The second half of Romans 6:23 says, "But the gift of God is eternal life in Christ Jesus our Lord." God loves us so much He did something about our rebellion. He sent His Son to pay the penalty for our sin so that we could be forgiven and have God's image in us restored.

What does the Word say? Read John 3:16. What is the result for those who receive God's free gift of salvation through Jesus?_____

_____

_____

What's your experience? Has there ever been a time when you received salvation through faith in Jesus Christ? If so, describe that experience.

_____

_____

_____

If you can't recall a time when you have received this gift and you would like to, pray this prayer. There is nothing magical about the words. God is listening to your heart.

Image Overhaul

Jesus, thank You for dying on the cross to pay the high price for the sins I have committed. I receive Your gift of salvation and invite you into my heart to be Lord and Savior of my life. Amen.

If you prayed this prayer, be sure that you tell a parent, church leader, or friend who is a Christian. The more support you get, the easier it will be for you to grow in your new relationship with Jesus.

☆ **Growing Means Depending on Him:** For Christians, growing means one thing—depending on His strength in our lives. This doesn't mean that we just sit back and wait on Him to make changes in us. Instead, we cooperate with Him as He changes us from the inside out. Fortunately, He has given us several tools to help us grow.

What does the Word say? Read 2 Peter 1:3–4. According to verse 3, how much of what we need to grow has He given us?

❑ Some of what we need
❑ Most of what we need
❑ None of what we need
❑ All of what we need

1. Prayer. As we pray about the different areas in our lives that need change, His power will change us little by little.

2. God's Word. According to verse 4, when we read and apply the promises from His Word, what two results can we expect? _____

_____

_____

Think about it: Do you take full advantage of prayer and God's Word to help you grow? Explain your answer. _____

_____

_____

_____

✔ **Try This:** Read John 3:30. The Christian life is the process of allowing God to become greater in our lives, while we become less. While it sounds simple, it's not at all easy. Take a few moments to make two lists. At the top of one, write the word "decrease." On this list write attitudes or actions that you want to diminish in your life. You may include things like selfishness, jealousy, or lust. Now write "increase" at the top of the second list. On this list include things that you want more of. Examples would be love, patience, or selflessness. Now transfer your list to a note card that you can tuck in your Bible. Pray over your list each day, asking God to help you as you seek for Him to increase his presence in your life. _____

_____

_____

_____

_____

Image Overhaul

_____

_____

✝ **Living the Word:** Read Colossians 3:10.

• When the Bible talks about "putting on the new self," it doesn't mean putting on a new outfit or even our alter ego. It simply means choosing to act in God's strength instead of our own. When we rely on Him, we find the power to obey.

• What are some practical things you can do to cooperate with God as He changes you from the inside out? _____

_____

_____

• Take a few moments to write a prayer thanking God that He doesn't leave you the way you are. Thank Him that He will remake you into His image as you trust and obey Him each day. _____

_____

_____

_____

_____

_____

_____

There is no better way
to understand the image of God
than to look at Jesus Christ.

We are children of God, and it has not appeared as yet what we will be. We know that when He appears, we will be like Him, because we will see Him just as He is.

1 John 3:2 NASB

Jesus—The Mirror Image of God

What is it with girls and mirrors? We just can't seem to stay away from them. Have you ever passed by a mirror and not at least glanced in it? Why is that? What are you thinking when you look at yourself in the mirror: *Girl, you're looking good today!* or, *Why did I ever leave the house?* Do you ever look in the mirror and think, *I am the image of God?* I would venture to say that this thought doesn't cross our minds very often—but it should.

In the last chapter, we saw that being created in the image of God is what makes human beings special. It's what sets humanity apart from the rest of God's creation and creatures. So when Ella's animal book says that humans belong to the same classification of animals as monkeys and apes, we know it is wrong because we are gloriously different from monkeys and apes. We, unlike other creatures, have the privilege and high calling of being in the very image of God.

Steaming Up God's Image

However, we also remember that because of humankind's sin, that image has been tarnished and distorted. Think about it this way. What happens to a mirror when you take a shower? It gets clouded over with steam. When you look in a steam-covered mirror, you can vaguely see your image, but the steam makes it difficult. It's frustrating to try to brush your hair when you can't see yourself.

That mirror has one purpose: to reflect your image. Why else does it take up wall space? But now, because of the steam, its ability to function as it was created is minimized. That steam is a picture of what sin does to our ability to image God. We are God's mirrors to the world, but when we are all steamed up with sin, God's image cannot be clearly seen in us.

Yet God has made a way for us to overcome the "steam" of sin. He started by sending His Son to show us what the image of God looks like. Then that perfect image died on the cross for the sins of those who willfully rejected the high calling of being the image of God. Through Jesus's sacrifice, the surface of our "mirror" is wiped clean so that we can, through faith in Christ, fulfill our purpose and beautifully reflect the image of God to the world.

Jesus—The Perfect Image of God

The main focus of this chapter is to look at Jesus as the image of God. As the Bible says, Christ is the "radiance of God's glory and the exact representation of his being" (Hebrews 1:3). The "radiance" that Christ gives off is not His own but the glory of God the Father. If you know anything about the moon, you know that the moon gives off no light of its own; it simply reflects the light of the sun. You might say that this is what the Son is to the Father. This is the "radiance" that Hebrews 1:3 is talking about.

The verse also says Christ is the "exact representation" of the Father. The word used here in the original language refers to "a stamp or impress, as on a coin or seal."[1] You've seen the impressions (designs) that are on coins: those impressions are made by a stamp that bears the image it produces. So when you look at a coin, you know exactly what the original stamp looks like. It's the same thing with Christ, the Son. When you look at Him, you can tell what the Father is like.[2]

Jesus—Showing Us How to Image God

When I was in college, I majored in opera. An important way for me to understand opera in its purest form was for my teachers to play videos and audios of the great opera singers. In the same way, God the Father has given us Jesus Christ as a visual example of the image of God. There is no better way to understand the image of God than to look at Jesus Christ. As Anthony Hoekema explains, "What we see and hear in Christ is what God intended for man."[3]

Me: God's Mirror to the World—Heather

Through the example of Jesus, we see how we can become radiant reflectors of God's image. In Luke 2:52, Luke writes that "Jesus grew in wisdom and stature, and in favor with God and men." Consider this verse. Luke is telling us how the young boy, Jesus of Nazareth, developed into the man who became the image of God. From this passage, we see that Jesus reflected the image of God at least four ways: mentally, physically, spiritually, and socially.

Mentally

First, as Luke 2:52 tells us, Jesus grew in "wisdom." Although Jesus was God and, as God, was all-knowing; as a human He grew mentally. As God's image bearers, humans are different from the animals because we have the ability to reason and learn in a way that sets us apart from all of God's other creatures. Commentator Wayne Grudem shares a great illustration of this point: "Beavers still build the same kind of dams they have built for thousands of generations, birds still build the same kind of nests, and bees still build the same kinds of hives. But we continue to develop greater skill in technology and . . . every field of endeavor."[4] In fact, as I write this, I use neither a quill nor a typewriter. I am using a computer. Imagine an ape developing the skill to invent a computer.

Jesus—The Mirror Image of God

Physically

Jesus also grew in "stature"—that is, Jesus grew physically. In a sense, our physical bodies teach us about God's attributes and how we are the image of God. I know what you might be thinking: *how does our physical body play a role in the image of God?* Think about it: our physical bodies give us the ability to see with our eyes. Grudem says,

> This is a Godlike quality because God Himself sees . . . although he does not do it with physical eyes like we have. Our ears give us the ability to hear, and this is a Godlike ability, even though God does not have physical ears. Our mouths give us the ability to speak, reflecting the fact that God is a God who speaks. Our senses of taste and touch and smell give us the ability to understand and enjoy God's creation, reflecting the fact that God himself understands and enjoys His creation.[5]

These physical attributes—our eyes, ears, mouth, etc.—teach us about God's own nature and help us understand how we are like Him.

Spiritually

Jesus also "grew in favor with God." Jesus grew spiritually. His life was "wholly directed toward God."[6] At the beginning of His ministry, though He was tempted by the devil, Jesus obeyed the Father. He often spent entire nights in prayer to the Father, and His prayers were for *God's* will, not His own. He once said, "My food . . . is to do the will of him who sent me and to finish his work"

(John 4:34). At the end of His earthly life, when Jesus was considering the suffering He was about to endure, He prayed, "My Father, if it is possible, may this cup be taken from me. Yet not as I will, but as you will" (Matthew 26:39).

Socially

Finally, Luke 2:52 tells us that Jesus "increased in favor . . . with God and men." In this we see that Jesus grew socially, or relationally. Jesus was completely focused on His neighbor.[7] When people who were in need of healing or food or forgiveness came to Him, He was always available to help them. In John 15:13, Jesus tells us about the greatest love of all: "Greater love has no one that this, that he lay down his life for his friends." This is the kind of love Jesus revealed as the supreme image of God.

Developing the Image of Christ

When I was growing up, the Polaroid was a popular camera. You would take a picture, and it would slowly develop into a clear snapshot. As Christians we are like a Polaroid snapshot. As God through His Spirit works in us, we slowly develop into people who look more like Jesus Christ, the perfect image of God.

What does all of this mean for you? How can you actually begin to look like Jesus? Well, you have to wait till the next chapter. But I will say that it is crucial that we understand how these truths impact our lives, because they are related to our purpose as human beings.

making it real

STUDY
GUIDE

Whose Reflection Do I See?

📖 **Opening Scripture:** Read Romans 8:29. Ask God to speak to you in a specific way as you study His Word today.

⭐ **God's Goal for Your Life:** Has anyone ever asked you to write goals for your life? Maybe a parent or guidance counselor encouraged you to really think about what you wanted to do in the future. Or you may have made yourself write goals for the school year or your summer break. Setting goals helps us stay on the right track and accomplish what we have set out to do. Did you know that God has a goal for your life?

What does the Word say? Reread Romans 8:29. According to this verse, what is God's goal for your life?

- ❏ To witness to my friends
- ❏ To be conformed to the likeness of Jesus
- ❏ To stop sinning
- ❏ To learn to sing

What do you think? Is God's goal for you also your goal for your life? Explain your answer. _____

_____

_____

While it's okay to have other ambitions for our lives, God's goal for us should be the overarching goal of everything else. You may aspire to

Whose Reflection Do I See?

be a veterinarian, doctor, or mom someday in the future, and that is great. But God wants you to be like Jesus as you fill those roles.

Think about it: What are some of the goals that you have for your future? In what ways can you reflect Christ as you meet those goals? _____

_____

_____

_____

⭐ **Is It You—or Him?** Take a few minutes to count how many mirrors you look in during the course of an average day. You'll want to count your bathroom mirror, the mirror you keep in your purse, your car mirror, and the one at school. You get the picture. Now let me ask you a question: what if the next time you looked in a mirror you saw someone else looking back at you? You would probably jump a mile in the air. It would be rather strange, don't you think? Well, did you know that when someone looks at you, the reflection they should see isn't you? They should see the reflection of Jesus living in you. Sure, they see you—but they should recognize that there is something different about you and the way you live your life. Let's look at four areas of life that God wants to remake into His image.

Fill in the blanks: Read Luke 2:52, and fill in the missing words.

"And Jesus grew in _____ and _____, and in _____ with _____ and _____."

Me: God's Mirror to the World—Study Guide

1. Mentally. If we are going to be changed into the image of Christ, we need to start with our minds. A wise person once said that what we think determines what we will become. That's why it's so important that we guard the things that we put into our minds.

What does the Word say? Read 2 Corinthians 10:5. What does this passage say that we should do with every thought? _____

_____

_____

What does it mean? What are some practical ways you can take your thoughts captive to Christ? _____

_____

_____

We are bombarded each day with all kinds of images and ideas that tempt us to lower our standards. The more we fill our minds with the trash of the world, the less our minds will become like Christ.

Think about it: How can you guard your mind against negative influences found on TV, the Internet, and music? _____

_____

_____

2. Physically. Obviously, our bodies are not going to look like Christ, but we can use our bodies in ways that honor Him.

What does the Word say? Read Romans 12:1. In what way can we worship God according to this passage? _____

Whose Reflection Do I See?

_____

_____

We can choose to honor God with our bodies or to dishonor Him. The little choices we make such as what we wear, what we eat, and how we act on a date should all reflect Christ.

What's your experience? Is there an action you participate in that does not honor God? If so, what steps can you take to change? _____

_____

_____

_____

_____

3. Spiritually. Just as Jesus spent time alone with His heavenly Father, we must spend time with Him as well. The more time we spend with Him, the more we will find that our desires change to love the things God loves and hate the things He hates.

Fill in the blanks: Read 2 Peter 3:18 and fill in the missing words.

"But _____ in the _____ and _____ of our Lord and Savior Jesus Christ."

What does it mean? Just as we cannot grow without physical nourishment, we absolutely will not grow unless we have spiritual food. God's Word is that food. The fact that you are taking the time to do this Bible study is a great way for you to grow spiritually. Keep it up, and you'll be amazed at the spiritual muscles He builds in you.

4. Socially. Galatians 5:13 says, "Serve one another in love." The biggest way that we reflect Christ to the world is by loving others with the love of God. The more you become like Christ, the more your life will be characterized by a selfless and loving attitude.

Think about it: In what ways can you practice serving others in love? In your family? Among your friends? How about to those less fortunate than you?

_____

_____

_____

Pray about it: Ask God to help you see others through the same eyes of love that He does. Next, make a list of people whom He has put in your life and called you to love. Pray that you will find tangible ways to serve them this week.

✝ **Living the Word:** Read 2 Corinthians 5:17, 21.

• What does verse 17 teach about who we are if we're Christians?

_____

_____

_____

• Whether or not you feel that it's true, you are a new creation in Christ. Write a short prayer thanking God for making you His new creation. _____

_____

Whose Reflection Do I See?

_____

_____

• Because of Jesus' death and resurrection, we can become the righteousness of Christ. How are you cooperating with Him as He remakes you? _____

_____

_____

_____

• Are there some changes you need to make so that you more radiantly reflect Jesus? If so, list them here. Next, share them with a trusted friend or mentor so she can pray with you as you rely on God's power to change._____

_____

_____

_____

_____

_____

The Christian self-image means understanding that your worth is found in your amazing dignity as God's image bearer.

> *But we all, with unveiled face, beholding*
> *as in a mirror the glory of the Lord, are being*
> *transformed into the same image from glory*
> *to glory, just as from the Lord, the Spirit.*
> 2 Corinthians 3:18 NASB

Beginning to Look a Lot Like Jesus

Does the name Terri Schiavo sound familiar? She was the woman who, in the spring of 2005, was in the middle of the right-to-die controversy. As I write this last chapter on the image of God, the breaking news is that Terri Schiavo died this morning, March 31, 2005, at the age of forty-one. She died at a hospice in Florida where she had resided for years while her husband and parents fought over her fate in the nation's longest, most bitter right-to-die dispute.[1]

A Distorted Image

How did we get to the point where a segment of our society no longer considers life sacred? How did the ones God created to mirror His image come to reflect such a distorted view?

This tragedy should not surprise us. After all, one of the most popular movies of 2005, *Million Dollar Baby*, promotes the right to die as a good thing.

Me: God's Mirror to the World—Heather

This film tells the story of Maggie Fitzgerald, a female fighter who becomes a champion in women's boxing. When Maggie suffers a terrible injury in the ring, she is paralyzed from the neck down. And when Maggie is confined to a wheelchair and a body she can't control, she decides she would rather die than accept her limitations. Eventually, her trainer, Frankie Dunn, decides to help Maggie take her own life.

Although the movie was billed as a fight film, it actually promotes the right to suicide. As film critic Michael Medved pointed out to Fox News's Bill O'Reilly, the narrator of the film describes the assisted suicide as "a heroic act to help somebody kill somebody else."[2]

Maggie Fitzgerald decided she did not want to live if living meant she could no longer be a boxing champion. Maggie tells Frankie, "I can't be like this, Boss, not after what I've done. I've seen the world. People chanted my name. I was in magazines."

The world-view of this film is the exact opposite of the Christian's understanding of the value of human life. True Christian love would help Maggie understand that she still possesses human dignity and gifts that could and should be used for the benefit of herself and others.

The Schiavo case reminds us that because of sin the truth about our dignity as humans created in the image of God has been distorted. Legal abortions and right-to-die cases are direct results of our society's failure to understand that humans are intended to reflect the image of God. Sin has steamed up their mirrors. When people misunderstand who they are, they cannot properly reflect God's image to the world. But in Christ the perfect image of God is restored (Colossians 1:15; Hebrews 1:3). And as the verse at the top of this chapter says, when Christians are transformed into the image of Christ, we mirror His glory.

The Practical Side of the Mirror

In the previous chapter, we saw that the image of God involves our whole person, including at least these four aspects: mental, physical, spiritual, and relational. In this chapter, I want to show how these different aspects affect our lives as Christians in practical ways.

Mentally

God has given us minds to *think*—rationally, logically, and creatively. Are you, as the image of God, using your mind as an instrument for the glory of God, or has your mirror become steamed up so that God's glory cannot be seen in you? The Bible says that to grow as a Christian, you must be "renewed in the spirit of your mind" (Ephesians 4:23 NASB). What this means is that in order to guard against being "conformed to this world," you must "be transformed by the renewing of your mind" (Romans 12:2 NASB) through constant time in the Word of God.

So, as I see it, my friend, you have a choice as to how to use your mind when it comes to living in this world. Let's briefly look at just three areas where these choices hit you often.

Entertainment. You can use the mind God gave you to apply godly wisdom when choosing the movies you see, the music you listen to, the Web sites you visit, and the books and magazines you read. Or you can be defined by accepting what pop culture says is okay or cool and hip or "hot." But remember, as you make your choices, you are the image of God.

Education. Since we are talking about the mind, I have to mention school. I know, I know, you think that you get it enough from your parents, but I have to say it. Knowing that your mental abilities serve to image God, use the brain God gave you to do your best in school. I didn't say that you have to make straight As, but you should strive for excellence and work as hard as you can. This is not an option for someone who understands this important call to live as the image of God.

Social judgments. When we see things happening in our culture like what happened to Terri Schiavo, we don't have to listen to what popular culture says about the issue. We should, instead, listen to what the Bible has to say on the matter. And the Bible clearly values *life*!

Physically

Our bodies play an important role in being the image of God. That is why Paul writes, "Glorify God in your body" (1 Corinthians 6:20 NASB). We talked in the last chapter about looking in the mirror and seeing ourselves as the image of God. Because we are in God's image, He wants us to treat our bodies with respect and honor.

Self-worth. I am amazed at how many young people today have a strong sense of self-hate. One day while walking in the mall, I was distressed to see a group of teenagers wearing really dark clothes, all hunched over, with enormous scowls on their faces. It saddened me so much, and I wondered what was going on in their heads. They had this look on their faces that communicated, *I am worthless* and *I hate my life.*

But then I realized that I have been guilty of jokingly saying, "I hate myself" when I've done something dumb and am mad at myself. But after I had Ella, I imagined her saying that to herself, and I made myself stop saying it, even in jest. God does not want me to hate myself; He created me in His image. You, too, are created in the image of God. You are of great worth in His sight.

Sexual purity. At our Girls of Grace conferences, we get lots of questions about sex (and we answer many of them in our new book, *Q&A*).[3] When we are sexually impure, we dishonor and disrespect the image of God. Now don't get me wrong. When God created Adam and Eve in His image, He blessed them and told them to "be fruitful and multiply, and fill the earth, and subdue it" (Genesis 1:28 NASB). Did you catch that? As the image of God, men and women are called to reproduce children, who also are the image of God. In other words, sex is instrumental in God's special plan for His creation. God invented sex! But as with so many things, the perversion of a good thing brings all kinds of trouble. And sex has been perverted in all kinds of ways.

There is the "normal" sexual perversion between boys and girls—and by "normal perversion," I mean sex outside of marriage, for this is definitely a perversion of God's plan. And beyond that, there is the perversion of homosexuality. Paul, when describing God's wrath against the sin of humankind, said, "Even the women turned against the natural way to have sex and instead indulged in sex with each other. And the men, instead of having normal sexual relationships with women, burned with lust for each other" (Romans 1:26–27 NLT).

From what Paul says in 1 Corinthians, we see that there's something about sexual sins that sets them apart from other sins: "No other sin so clearly affects the body as this one does. For sexual immorality is a sin against your own body (6:18 NLT). He goes on to explain that one of the things that makes sexual sin different for believers is that our bodies are the home of the Holy Spirit, and our bodies have been bought with a price. When we sin sexually, we violate the Holy Spirit living in us. Paul concludes by saying, "Honor God with your body" (v. 20 NLT).

Sexual purity is not up for debate. Homosexuality and sex outside of marriage are not included in God's plan for us. They are wrong and sinful and, as a result, very costly.

Cutting. Another question that we've been asked about at every conference is cutting. This is a growing trend among teenagers. If you are one of those girls who cuts herself to feel better inside, I want you to imagine that I am sitting right across from you, holding both your hands in mine, looking straight into your eyes.

Here is what I want to say: "I know that you must be experiencing something very painful inside to want to cause yourself pain, but cutting yourself is not a solution. When you hurt yourself, you are also hurting God. He knows your pain, and He alone is the solution to relieving that pain. If you need forgiveness, He can give it to you. If you need comfort, He can give it to you. If you need direction, He is the Way. And if you need to be saved, He is the last stop. Cling to God, and trust Him with your life. God created your body for His purposes. The only way to overcome your pain is to begin the process of living your life with the full awareness and intention of being God's image bearer physically, mentally, spiritually, and relationally."

Spiritually

God made us as His image bearers, and He has implanted within us a deep capacity to know Him intimately. This intimacy begins with a personal relationship with Jesus Christ.

The relationship begins. Our relationship with Christ begins with a rebirth. John 3:5 says that in order to be a part of God's kingdom, we must be born again by the Spirit of God. As we place our faith in the Lord Jesus Christ, who is the perfect image of God, we are united to Him. We are now "in Christ." So the perfect image that was damaged by our sin begins the process of being renewed through Christ (Colossians 3:10). Our conversion to Christ is made possible by God's amazing grace.

The relationship grows. After we are born into God's family, we have a responsibility to grow in the grace and knowledge of our Lord Jesus Christ (2 Peter 3:18). This means you need to be active in your church, studying and applying your Bible, serving your fellow human beings, and saying no to sinful temptations. In fact, Scripture says we should "flee from youthful lusts and pursue righteousness, faith, love and peace, *with those* who call on the Lord from a pure heart" (2 Timothy 2:22 NASB).

The relationship deepens. We take our relationship with Christ to a deeper level as we create an atmosphere of holiness in our lives. Sounds hard, doesn't it? Living a life of holiness isn't easy. When I invite company to my house, I try to create an atmosphere that will make them feel at home. I make sure my house is clean, a good meal is prepared, and candles are burning that give off a sweet-smelling aroma.

In the same way, we need to create an atmosphere in our lives that will make our Lord Jesus Christ at home in our hearts. Don't you realize how short our lives are in light of eternity? Scripture says, "All flesh is like grass, and all its glory like the flower of grass. The grass withers, and the flower falls off " (1 Peter 1:24 NASB). This means that it is foolish to pursue our own agendas. After all, our glory is "like the flower of grass," which dies out every winter. Girls, we need to be pursuing something deeper and more enduring than that. Our purpose is to bring glory to God (Isaiah 43:7). We do this as we grow spiritually and are conformed to the image of Christ (Romans 8:29).

Relationally

God is a relational God. He is the Father, the Son, and the Holy Spirit. These three persons of the Godhead are in perfect communion with one another and make up the one true God. God didn't *need* a relationship with us, but He *wanted* a relationship with us. He created us to be the same way. We need the fellowship of other believers. It is vital in our walk with God. I can even see it already in my six-month-old son, Nate. He is so happy when he is surrounded by his mommy or daddy or even his big sister, Ella. But the minute we walk away, he cries. He already has the need for fellowship. Walking with God requires Christian community. Here's some of what that means for you.

Choose godly friends. Do you have godly friends who will encourage you and hold you accountable? The kind of friends you have is *so* important. You've probably heard the scripture a hundred times, but it's still true: "Bad company corrupts good character" (1 Corinthians 15:33). Who you hang out with really does matter, so choose your friends wisely and with your role as God's mirror in mind.

Treat others kindly. How do you treat others? Both friends and strangers are created in God's image. Furthermore, do you treat people who are different from you or people who annoy you with grace and love? It's not always easy. When I'm driving in my car and someone cuts me off, I can become a different person. I heard someone say one time that when she is behind the wheel, the fruit of the Spirit falls right off her tree.

I'm sometimes guilty of not seeing other people as the image of God. If I did, I would treat them kindly even when they don't treat me right. After all, all persons were created to be the image of God. In fact, Scripture says it is wrong to speak evil of others for the very reason that we are made in the image of God (James 3:9). Girls, wouldn't it remove a lot of stress from your lives if you refused to take part in conversations that are demeaning to others? Treating others kindly in what you say will take you a long way toward mirroring God to others.

Date wisely. If you image God in your relationships, this should play a dominant role in the kind of relationships you build with guys. I've been there, and I know what many of you think: *He is such a nice guy, and he is so cute! I can help him in the spiritual area.* Girls, God never calls us to missionary date. Your relationships play a vital role in imaging God, and so these relationships must be built primarily on a mutual love for God and His Christ. Scripture says, "Do not be bound together with unbelievers; for what partnership have righteousness and lawlessness, or what fellowship has light with darkness?" (2 Corinthians 6:14 NASB).

Becoming God's Image Bearer

A healthy self-image does not mean feeling good about yourself on the basis of your looks, achievements, or behavior. The Christian self-image means looking at yourself in the light of God's work of forgiveness and renewal in your life. It means understanding that your worth is found in your amazing dignity as God's image bearer in all aspects: mentally, spiritually, physically, and relationally.

Look in the mirror and smile; you are a beautiful creation of a creative God. And what do you know—you are beginning to bear a striking resemblance.

making it real

Choosing to Believe the Truth

📖 **Opening Scripture:** Begin by reading 2 Corinthians 5:21. Ask God to teach you from His Word today.

⭐ **Rethink Who You Are:** If you've turned on the TV lately, you've seen the lineup of makeover shows that are popular with viewers. The show's producers usually pick someone who suffers from low self-esteem and then make her over. They give her new teeth, updated clothes, a cuter nose, and a different body. It's like she was a frog, and now she's a princess. You would think that this girl's whole life would change overnight. But did you know that many times it doesn't turn out that way? The woman who had the makeover may look different on the outside, but she feels the same way on the inside. Why? Because unless we change our thoughts, we'll feel like the same old us. It's the same way with growing in the Christian life. Until we start to believe that what God's Word says is true about us, we'll feel like the same old sinners destined to make the same old mistakes.

What does the Word say? Reread 2 Corinthians 5:21. God made Jesus to become what for us? _____

_____

Because of that, what benefit is ours? _____

_____

Choosing to Believe the Truth

_____

_____

What's your experience? If you're a Christian, then in Christ you can become the righteousness of God. Have you ever come to a point where you really understood that truth and let it change your life? If so, explain. If not, write a prayer asking God to help you begin to grasp that truth. _____

_____

_____

_____

_____

Just as those who have had a makeover, we need to retrain our minds to think about who we truly are. The more we grow in our relationship with Him, the more we act like who He's made us to be.

⭐ **The Power of Your Mind:** Your mind truly is the most amazing creation. It has such great power for your good and also for your harm. What you think determines so much of who you become. Have you ever stopped to think about this before? If you constantly think, *I am stupid,* you will never live up to your full potential. If you let your mind believe that, you'll never overcome a habit; you'll live in slavery to that habit for the rest of your life. It's only when we change our negative thinking and replace it with the truth of God's Word that we can break free from the lies that run through our minds.

Me: God's Mirror to the World—Study Guide

What does the Word say? Read Romans 8:5–6. Those who have the Spirit of God, meaning Christians, are to set their minds on what? _____

_____

_____

What is the result? _____

Think about it: Has there ever been a time when you focused your mind on God and His Word and experienced His peace? If so, explain.

_____

_____

What does it mean? What do you think this verse means by "the mind set on the flesh is death"? _____

_____

_____

Left to our own direction, or our flesh, our minds can lead us down a dangerous path. That's why it's crucial that we continually renew our minds in God's Word. We can believe anything, whether or not it's true, when we stop running our thoughts through the filter of the Bible. We must constantly guard our minds from the lies that bombard us each day.

Fill in the blanks: Read Philippians 4:6–7 and fill in the missing words.

"Do _____ be anxious about _____, but in _____, by _____ and petition, with thanksgiving, present your _____ to _____. And the _____ of God, which transcends all understanding, will _____ your _____ and your _____ in Christ Jesus."

Did you see it? There's that word *peace* again. When our minds are yielded to Him, we'll find that most wonderful gift: peace. People would pay millions for it, but money can't buy it. True peace can only be found when we look to God.

☆ **Replace the Lies with Truth:** Maybe you have believed some lies about yourself, and you're tired of living under the weight of those lies. Let's look at three practical steps we can take to replace the lies with truth.

1. Identify the lies. Take some time to think about some of the things you believe about yourself. Maybe you think that you are a dirty sinner who is unworthy of God's love. If so, remember that our opening verse told us that He loved you so much that He died so you could become His righteousness. Maybe you struggle with cutting, like Heather talked about, and you think that the only way to deal with your stress is by hurting yourself. That is a lie! God will help you manage your stress as you rely on Him and His power to change.

Pray about it: Take some time to ask God to show you some of the lies you believe that contradict what He says about you. Write them here.

_____

_____

_____

_____

_____

2. Pray. Now take your list of lies and bring them to God. Agree with Him that these are not true and that you want to replace them with the truth of His Word. Ask Him to give you verses that contradict the lies that you have believed. The more time you spend talking and listening to Him, the more you will start to recognize His voice of truth speaking into your life.

What does the Word say? Read John 14:6. In what three ways does Jesus describe Himself in this verse? _____

_____

To overcome the lies, we must continually draw closer to Jesus, who is the Truth.

3. Battle the lies with truth. After we have identified the lies we believe and have prayed about them, then we need to find the ammunition to battle them. Can you guess what our weapon is? You guessed it: the Word of God.

Fill in the blanks: Read Psalm 119:160 and fill in the missing words.

"All your _____ are _____; all _____ righteous _____ are _____."

If you want to battle feelings that you aren't loved, find verses that tell about His unfailing love. If you struggle with thinking you are destined to fail, find verses about God's strength. Then write them out and learn them. Memorize them, and make them a part of your natural thought process. Consider them your mental chewing gum. While you're exercising, think of these verses. While you take a shower, let the truth wash over you. Before long, you will find that the lies you believed have been replaced. Gradually, you will find that it's easier to believe what God says about you.

✔ **Try This:** Look back at the list of lies you are tempted to believe. Now pick one of those lies. Spend some time looking for verses that contradict that lie, and write them in the space provided. You may want to use the concordance in the back of your Bible to help you. Be patient. It may take some time, but as you look, you'll be amazed at how God leads you to just the right verse for your particular struggle. _____

_____

_____

_____

_____

_____

Me: God's Mirror to the World—Study Guide

✝ **Living the Word:** Read Colossians 3:2.

• What do you think this verse means by setting our minds on things above? _____

_____

_____

• What are some earthly things that steal our mind's attention from thinking about the things of God? _____

_____

_____

• What are some practical steps you can take to set your mind on things above? _____

_____

_____

_____

_____

_____

_____

Notes to *Girls of Grace, Make It Real*

Mouth Management

1. Frank Peretti, *No More Bullies: For Those Who Wound or Are Wounded* (Nashville: W Publishing Group, 2003), 116.

2. Ibid., 150; emphasis in original.

Sanctified Gossip

1. Peretti, *No More Bullies,* 153.

If the Shoe Fits, Wear It!

1. Rick Warren, *The Purpose Driven Life* (Grand Rapids: Zondervan, 2002), 251.

2. Florence Littauer, *Personality Plus: How to Understand Others by Understanding Yourself* (Grand Rapids: Revell, revised 1992).

Dirty Laundry

1. Cynthia Spell Humbert, *Deceived by Shame, Desired by God* (Colorado Springs: NavPress, 2001).

Notes

Reflections of a Better Me

1. Wayne Grudem, *Systematic Theology* (Grand Rapids: Zondervan, 1995), 444.

2. Anthony A. Hoekema, *Created in God's Image* (Grand Rapids: Eerdmans, 1986), 72.

3. Ibid., 85.

Jesus—The Mirror Image of God

1. W. E. Vine, "Image," *An Expository Dictionary of New Testament Words* (Old Tappan, N.J.: Revell, 1940; reprint 1966), 247.

2. Hoekema, *God's Image*, 21.

3. Ibid., 22.

4. Grudem, *Systematic Theology*, 446.

5. Ibid., 448.

6. Hoekema, *God's Image,* 74.

7. Ibid.

Beginning to Look a Lot Like Jesus

1. "Terri Schiavo Dies, but Battle Continues," MSNBC news service report, March 31, 2005, www.msnbc.msn.com/id/7293186/ (accessed April 12, 2005).

2. Al Mohler, "Million Dollar Baby—Assisted Suicide at the Oscars," www.crosswalk.com/news/weblogs/mohler/?adate=2/24/2005#1314506 (accessed April 12, 2005).

3. Point of Grace, *Girls of Grace, Q&A* (West Monroe, La.: Howard, 2005).

other Girls of Grace products

Point of Grace, along with Nancy Alcorn, answers questions collected from previous Girls of Grace conferences about family, faith, sex, dating, friendships, themselves, and more.

Start your day off right, with this fun and spiritually uplifting book, which has 52 devotionals from Point of Grace—one for each week of the year. It's the perfect way to make sure you are centered on God and ready for whatever your day brings.

With plenty of space for journaling, each page also has an extra bit of encouragement, through scriptures, quotes from the Point of Grace members, and inside and outside beauty tips.

This easy-to-use DVD has been carefully designed so that anyone can facilitate a dynamic group session. Bringing the Point of Grace members right into your church or home study groups, viewers will be uplifted, encouraged, and brought closer to God.

HOWARD BOOKS
A DIVISION OF SIMON & SCHUSTER
www.howardpublishing.com

Notes from Your Heart

Notes from Your Heart

Notes from Your Heart

_____

_____

_____

_____

_____

_____

_____

_____

_____

_____

_____

_____

_____

_____

_____

_____

_____

_____

_____

_____

_____

_____

_____

_____

_____

_____

_____

_____

_____

Notes from Your Heart

_____

_____

_____

_____

_____

_____

_____

_____

_____

_____

_____

_____

_____

_____

_____

_____

_____

_____

_____

_____

_____

_____

_____

_____

_____

_____

_____

_____

Notes from Your Heart

Notes from Your Heart

Notes from Your Heart

Notes from Your Heart

_____
_____
_____
_____
_____
_____
_____
_____
_____
_____
_____
_____
_____
_____
_____
_____
_____
_____
_____
_____
_____
_____
_____
_____
_____
_____
_____

Notes from Your Heart

Notes from Your Heart

Notes from Your Heart